PART I

The Political and Historical Determinants of the Medical Care Sector in Great Britain from 1911 to 1974

CHAPTER I

The Political Determinants of the National Health Insurance Act of 1911

INTRODUCTION

In the search for documents, reports, pieces of legislation and the like which preceded and affected the implementation of the National Health Service (NHS) in 1948, one finds that both the National Health Insurance Act of 1911 and the Dawson Report of 1920 occupy a prominent position in medical history literature and are considered to have, to a large degree, influenced the present structure of the NHS. In such literature, moreover, both events are generally attributed to the *noblesse oblige* attitude of the British aristocracy, as well as to its presumed administrative genius.[1] And in each case, an idealist interpretation of social change is presented, i.e., it is assumed that the well intended and socially motivated values supposedly embodied in the upper classes are the motor forces of history.

Due to the importance that these two documents and the forces that determined them have for understanding the present distribution and composition of resources in the NHS, let me focus on each, providing an alternative explanation for its appearance on the political horizon. Indeed, rather than emanating from the attributed *noblesse oblige*, administrative genius, foresight, or whatever, of the British upper class and aristocracy, I believe that the National Health Insurance Act, as well as the Dawson Report, emerged in response to specific economic and political forces, forces that were generated by a conflict between social classes and fractions of these classes that took place during and after the Industrial Revolution in Britain. So that we can better understand the nature of these conflicts, let us begin by briefly describing the economic base of Britain at the end of the nineteenth and the beginning of the twentieth centuries, and the class structure and relations that it determined.

The Economic and Social Transformation of Britain at the End of the Nineteenth and the Beginning of the Twentieth Centuries

The main characteristics of the transformation of the British economy during the late nineteenth and early twentieth centuries were:[2]

1. a dramatic decline in agricultural production, which fell from more than one-third of the national product in the first decade of the nineteenth century to about 6% by the first decade of the twentieth;
2. an increase in the share of mining and manufacturing, from less than a quarter at the beginning of the nineteenth century to over 40% of the total national product by the end of that century; and
3. an increase in the share represented by transport and trade, particularly in the second half of the nineteenth century.

These changes in the sectors of the economy were also reflected in the composition of the labour force, briefly outlined in Table 1.1. As the table indicates, the percentage of the labour force in agriculture steadily declined, while there were dramatic increases in the manufacture / mining and trade / transport sectors.

These changes reflect the shift from agricultural to industrial capitalism. It is interesting to note that while in France the change from one mode of production to another required a political revolution — the French Revolution — no such profound political change (reflecting a conflict between the feudal aristocracy and the industrial bourgeoisie) took place in Britain. That peculiarity of the English was due to the fact that in Britain the landed nobility and gentry were themselves the ones who invested in new forms of enterprises at crucial

TABLE 1.1 *Estimated Percentage Distribution of the British Labour Force, 1801–1911 (as percentages of the total occupied population)*

Year	*Agriculture, Forestry, Fishing*	*Manufacture, Mining, Industry*	*Trade and Transport*	*Domestic and Personal*	*Professional and Public*	*Total*
1801	35.9	29.7	11.2	11.5	11.8	100%
1851	21.7	42.9	15.8	13.0	6.7	100%
1901	8.7	46.3	21.4	14.1	9.6	100%
1911	8.3	46.4	21.5	13.9	9.9	100%

Source: Deane and Cole, *op. cit*., p. 142.

periods of capitalist transformation and absorbed the new entrants from trade and finance in each generation. The bourgeoisie thus was not an independent class from the aristocracy. Rather, it was a successor and willing partner to the aristocracy, which remained dominant in that relationship.[3]

Together, they constituted the upper class — the owners of land and capital — representing, according to Cole and Postgate,[4] less than 2% of the population. Also, and emerging with the Industrial Revolution, there were the middle classes or petty bourgeoisie, including primarily professionals, skilled craftsmen, tradesmen, and small entrepreneurs.

At the other extreme of the social spectrum, there were: (1) the working class, a nascent force which grew very substantially in terms of numbers during and after the Industrial Revolution, with the better organized and most highly unionized sectors of that class including textile, steel, transport, and coal mining workers; (2) the peasantry or agricultural workers, whose numbers dwindled quite dramatically as a result of rapid changes in land ownership, with large farms taking over small ones and thus stimulating the migration of agricultural workers to the cities; and (3) the subproletariat, which included the unemployed and the unemployable, and which, for long periods of time, represented a large sector of the British population.[5]

Class Structure in the Health Sector

An awareness of this class structure is of paramount importance in understanding both the distribution as well as the composition of the medical profession, not only at that time, but also today. Indeed, at the beginning of this century, we find the class structure and hierarchy replicated in the health sector. At the very top were the physicians and surgeons, of upper class origin and with the advantage of a university education.[6] These men (women were practically absent from the medical profession) primarily served the urban rich, and only secondarily the hospitalized poor, who provided the teaching material for the centres of learning, i.e. voluntary hospitals controlled by the upper class. Their professional organization was the Royal College of Physicians, an exclusive association which regulated the jobs and positions in the voluntary hospitals. (Even today, the Royal Colleges regulate the jobs and positions in the NHS hospitals.) Established by Henry VIII, the Royal College of Physicians legitimized the power of wealthy individuals to provide care for the British aristocracy and furthermore, provided them with a monopoly over that power. It is interesting to note that the political economist, Adam Smith, found such corporate monopolism to be unjustifiable, advocating that anyone should be free to practise medicine and that it should be left to the consumer to judge who is or isn't a good doctor. The response of the Royal College to this was, in the words of Lord Cowen, that 'the community is rarely able to judge . . . of the merits of medical men . . . The life and health of a great proportion of mankind are in the hands of ignorant people . . . The legislature should take special care that the necessary art should, as far as possible, be rendered both safe and useful to society.'[7]

The other group of health professionals — the majority — encompassed the apothecaries and general practitioners, who served (1) sectors of the emerging middle class: they were forced to compete for this limited clientele, under very unsatisfactory conditions, with the surgeons and physicians in the outpatient departments of voluntary hospitals and were paid by these clients on a fee-for-service basis; (2) large sectors of the growing working class, organized into sick societies and fraternities: in this case, they were paid either by capitation or by salary; and (3) the subproletariat and the poor in the much hated Poor Law hospitals: here they were paid, for the most part, by salary or capitation, and worked under conditions of clear exploitation. It is interesting to note that both Forsyth[8] and Tudor Hart[9] attribute the hostility that existed on the part of the general practitioners towards the local authorities prior to and during the NHS to conditions in the Poor Law hospitals during this period.

In summary, then, the lines of demarcation between these groups — physicians and surgeons on the one hand, and apothecaries and general practitioners on the other — stemmed primarily from the different social class origins of the two categories of doctors, as well as from the distinct class composition of the groups treated by each branch of the profession,[10] i.e., at the top, the upper class doctor serving the upper class, and, at the bottom, the apothecaries serving the working class and the poor, with both groups competing on a rather unequal basis for the emerging middle class clientele. The second group of doctors was clearly on the short end of the competition. Indeed, the working conditions and prestige of the apothecaries and general practitioners were very poor. Bernard Shaw, with his characteristic wit, put it quite bluntly, writing that:

> To make matters worse, doctors [general practitioners] are hideously poor . . . Better be a railway porter than an ordinary English practitioner.

> To secure the vehement and practically unanimous support of the rank and file of the medical profession for any sort of treatment or operation, all that is necessary is that it can be easily practiced by a rather shabbily dressed man in a dirty house without any assistance and that the materials for it shall cost, say, a penny.[11]

In summary, then, class structure reproduced itself in the medical sector, with two types of physicians for two classes of citizens. To understand the present structure and composition of the medical profession, it is necessary to keep this historical note in mind.

Class Conflict and Class Alliances: Their Implications in the Health Sector

The changes in the mode of production brought about by the Industrial Revolution determined a considerable growth of the middle and working classes, with a subsequent growth in their political power. And both classes allied in the second half of the nineteenth century to challenge and counteract the still predominant power of the upper class or aristocracy.

This alliance took place in the health sector as well, with a slow but steady growth in the power of general practice. This growth of power determined two main demands: (1) a demand for unification of the medical profession, and (2) a monopolization of practice and organization. The demand for unification of the medical profession was resisted by the surgeons and physicians — the upper strata within that profession. Indeed,

> the debates on the medical reform and unification of the medical profession were long tinged with arguments about the necessity to preserve an inferior order of practitioner to meet the needs of the lower classes. The view ot general practice as the lowest order in the medical world persisted long after the statutory decision to unify the profession.[12]

Still, the alliance of the general practitioners with the middle classes (whose political arm — the Liberal Party — controlled the government) determined the passage in Parliament of the 1858 Medical Act — an Act that unified the medical profession, at least in theory, with the establishment of the General Medical Council. By guaranteeing the quality of the profession, the Council was supposed to safeguard the interests of the state and of the public.[13] It was — and still is today — the function of that Council to register the duly recognized practitioners, setting the standards to be observed by the educational and licensing institutions, and also providing mechanisms for examining the public's complaints. In practice, through its regulation of entry into the profession, the Council functioned within the medical field as a professional 'birth control pill'. Consequently, it had a dramatic effect on the number of practitioners, which declined from 30,000 physicians in 1841 to 11,000 qualified ones in 1858.[14]

It is interesting to note that while these measures did improve the situation of the general practitioners, nonetheless the distribution of power and prestige within the profession remained unchanged. Indeed, in much the same way that the upper class was forced to make some concessions to the emerging middle classes (although without substantially relinquishing its dominance in both economic and social life), similarly in the medical profession, the physicians / surgeons had to make some concessions to accommodate the newly emerging power of the practitioners. But this accommodation did little either to change the power relations within the medical profession — general practitioners continued to enjoy less power and prestige — or to alter that profession's patterns of control. Indeed, the General Medical Council was practically controlled then — as it is today — by the upper class physicians and surgeons, the members of the Royal College of Physicians and Surgeons.

Having described the class structure and relations of Great Britain and their implications in the practice of medicine, let me now explain the genesis of the National Health Insurance Act of 1911 (and later, that of the Dawson Report). And we shall see that this class structure and the relations it determines form the scenario essential for a full understanding of subsequent events.

The Class Struggle: Political Origins of the National Health Insurance Act

A main characteristic of the second half of the nineteenth and beginning of the twentieth century was the dramatic growth of the working class and, subsequently, of the trade union movement. The following figures demonstrate the degree of that growth. In 1885, less than 10% of the adult, male, manual labour force was organized into effective unions. By 1892, however, this figure had doubled, with the total number of union members being 1½ million in that year, 2 million in 1905, and 4 million in 1914.[15]

But equally important was the simultaneous change in the composition and leadership of this labour movement, with predominance shifting away from the craft and textile unions towards the newly emerging coalminers, dockers and railway workers — casually referred to as the Triple Alliance. This Alliance was far more militant than the earlier union movement had been, and also more receptive to the socialist ideas that were spreading all over Europe. These ideas were transmitted to the labour movement by the Fabians, the Christian Socialists, and by the most radical and influential force of all — the Social Democratic Federation, which joined Marx in the First International. This militancy was reflected in a rising number of strikes, with strike activity reaching a peak during and after the economic depression of 1890-1893.[16]

Moreover, this atmosphere of social unrest was heightened by the general unrest prevalent in Continental Europe, brought about by the first Soviet Revolution — the unsuccessful October Revolution of 1905 — and other uprisings, particularly in Germany. The spectre of revolutionary socialism was lurking behind the scenes, alarming the upper and even middle classes.[17] Concessions had to be made. And in the health sector, the need to respond to that social unrest led first to the National Health Insurance Act of 1911 and later on to the Dawson Report.

Indeed, the Liberal Government, representing, at that time, the enlightened sectors of the upper and middle classes, viewed the enactment of social legislation as the best strategy for stopping the spread of socialism. In the words of Balfour, in 1895,

> Social legislation is not merely to be distinguished from Socialist legislation, but it is its most direct opposite and its most effective antidote.[18]

Thus, and contrary to prevalent interpretation, the social legislation enacted in this period did not have anything to do with the *noblesse oblige* of the aristocracy or of the nascent bourgeoisie for that matter. The main reasons for that legislation were: first, the social demands by labour for increased wages, improved working conditions (primarily shortened working hours), and strengthened job protection and security; and, second, the social needs of the capitalist class, which was forced to deliver the demanded goods and services in order to co-opt and / or calm the unsettled labour battlefront, and also to increase productivity by cutting down on absenteeism due to sickness. Actually, the Liberal Party used both these arguments to convince its constituency to support the National Health Insurance Act. Regarding the latter one, the poor physical condition of the working class — shown by the large number of young workers (48% of potential soldiers) who could not be recruited as soldiers for the Boer War because of poor health — awakened the upper class to the necessity for a healthy labour force and a healthy Army.[19]

It is interesting to note, however, that while the working class was able to trigger a response to its demands, it was not able to have its programme implemented. Rather, the response to working class pressure was to take place strictly within the parameters determined by the class in power. For example, the demands of the labour movement included the call for nationalization of the means of production, including state provision of services (which encompassed health services). This demand for nationalization was particularly strong after World War I, and has persisted to this day in the famous Clause 4 of the Labour Party's Constitution, expressing the Labour Party's commitment to nationalization. And part of this demand at that time — post-W.W.I — was that health services should be paid for out of general revenues, and not through premiums or social security payrolls. In terms of administration, a demand existed (and was articulated by the Webbs) that health services should be administered by local authorities.[20]

The Liberals, however, strongly opposed such schemes for a nationalized health sector. Using arguments quite similar to the ones that are being put forward today in the U.S. by conservative and liberal circles, the Liberals indicated that the economy could not afford such nationalized services. Instead, they maintained that the state should intervene to ensure the capability of the workers (but not their dependents) to buy ambulatory (but not hospital) medical services. The main strategy was considered to be more one of income maintenance than of the provision of health services. In terms of funding, the Liberal Government envisioned health insurance as being supported not from general revenues, but on a flat rate basis between employee, employer and government, with benefits graduated according to income.[21] And in terms of administration, they felt that the already voluntary insurance companies — primarily the powerful commercial insurers — should administer the national scheme. This decision was, as Forsyth indicates, a triumph for the commercial insurance interests.[22] Moreover, complementary to the compulsory insurance for all workers earning less than £2 a week, they suggested the creation of a voluntary insurance that would primarily cover workers' dependents. Due to pressures from the British Medical Association to keep the upper limit of those entitled to medical benefits as low as possible, and to provide for medical representation in the administration of the national insurance, this scheme had to be somewhat modified later to take into account the professional, as well as insurance interests.[23]

Thus, it was primarily the social unrest, so widespread in the working class, that forced the British establishment to take steps to enact ameliorative legislation. The form that this response took, however, was clearly attuned to the specific interests of those groups within that British establishment — commercial insurance and the medical profession — that were most likely to be affected by the implementation of such social legislation.

To sum up, a process occurred in this period that has repeated itself in many Western capitalist countries since then. That is, there emerges a popular demand for assuring the availability of services on the one hand, and the capacity to pay for them on the other. And that demand eventually determines a response from the dominant class, a response based on the necessity for that class to legitimate the social order in which it holds dominance. And that dominance further reflects itself in the nature of the response, i.e., it primarily mirrors and reproduces the class interests and ideology of that dominant class. But this is not a sufficient explanation for the final shape of the response. Indeed, once the response has been triggered and its class character established, the specific interest groups, including, among others, professional interests, creep in and substantially shape its final form.[24] This is, in fact, exactly what has happened throughout most of the history of health legislation — from the Lloyd George Act of 1911 to the 1968 establishment of Medicare in the U.S.

NOTES

1 Both Lipset and Anderson consider the *noblesse oblige* morality, supposedly inherent in the aristocracy, to have been a primary determinant of social change in Britain, both at the end of the nineteenth and the beginning of the twentieth centuries. See, for example, S. M. Lipset, *The First New Nation: The United States in Historical and Comparative Perspective,* New York, Basic Books (1963); and O. Anderson, *Health Care: Can There Be Equity? The United States, Sweden, and England,* New York, John Wiley and Sons (1972), p. 93.

2 P. Deane and W. A. Cole, *British Economic Growth, 1688-1959,* London, Cambridge University Press (1967), p. 168.

3 The transition from agricultural to industrial capitalism in Great Britain and its subsequent effect on the class relations of twentieth-century Britain have been the subject of much debate among Marxist historians, not only in Great Britain but in Continental Europe as well. See, for example, P. Anderson, 'Origins of the Present Crisis', *New Left Review*, 23 (1964); T. Nairn, 'The English Working Class', *New Left Review*, 24 (1964); E. P. Thompson, 'The Peculiarities of the English', in R. Miliband and J. Saville (eds.), *The Socialist Register*, London, Merlin Press (1965); and N. Poulantzas, 'Marxist Political Theory in Great Britain', *New Left Review*, 43 (1968).

4 G. D. H. Cole and R. Postgate, *The British Common People, 1746-1946,* London, Methuen (1961).

5 For a discussion of the class and occupational structure of the British population, see J. Kuczynski, *A Short History of Labour Conditions Under Industrial Capitalism, Volume I,* London, Frederick Muller Ltd. (1942).

6 A. M. Carr-Saunders and P. A. Wilson, *The Professions, Part I,* Oxford, Clarendon (1933), p.65.

7 L. Cowen, 'Liberty, Laissez-Faire and Licensure in Nineteenth-Century Britain', *Bulletin of the History of Medicine,* 43 (Jan-Feb. 1969), p. 31. See also J. R. Lee, *Life of Adam Smith*, New York, Augustus M. Kelley (1965), pp. 273-280; and J. L. Berlant, *Profession and Monopoly. A Study of Medicine in the United States and Great Britain*, Berkeley, University of California Press (1975), pp. 128-176.

8 G. Forsyth, *Doctors and State Medicine: A Study of the British Health Service,* New York, J. B. Lippincott Co. (1966).

9 J. Tudor Hart, 'Primary Care in the Industrial Areas of Britain', *International Journal of Health Services,* 2 (August 1972), p. 349.

10 D. G. Gill, 'The British National Health Service: Professional Determinants of Administrative Structure', *International Journal of Health Services,* 1 (November 1971), p. 342.

11 G. B. Shaw, *The Doctor's Dilemma*, London, Constable (1930), p. 25.

12 J. Brotherston, 'Evolution of Medical Practice', in G. McLachlan and T. McKeown (eds.), *Medical History and Medical Care*, Oxford, Oxford University Press (1971), p. 91.

13 Gill, *op. cit.*, p. 344.

14 *Ibid.*

15 Kuczynski, *op. cit.*

16 *Ibid.*, p. 103 and p. 106.

17 W. Abendroth, *A Short History of the European Working Class,* New York, Monthly Review Press (1972).

18 Quoted in V. George and P. Wilding, 'Social Values, Social Class, and Social Policy', *Social and Economic Administration,* 6(3) (1972), pp. 236-248.

19 Mentioned in R. Levitt, *The Reorganized National Health Service,* London, Holmes and Meier (1976), p. 12. Also, see B.B. Gilbert, *The Evolution of National Insurance in Great Britain. The Origins of the Welfare State,* London, Michael Joseph (1976).

20 See, for example, the *Minority Report* (written by Beatrice Webb) of the Royal Commission on the Poor Laws and the Relief of Distress of 1909. London. Her Majesty's Stationery Office, Command Paper 4499 (1909).

21 G. Forsyth, 'Introduction', in J. Van Langendonck, *Prelude to Harmony on a Community Theme. Health Care Insurance Policies in the Six and Britain,* Oxford, Oxford University Press (1975), p. 8.

22 *Ibid.*

23 Gill, *op. cit.*, p. 346.

24 For a further elaboration of this point, see V. Navarro, 'Social Class, Political Power and the State and their Implications in Medicine', *op. cit.*

CHAPTER II

The Dawson Report: The Conservative Response to a Socialist Threat

INTRODUCTION: REGIONALIZATION AND THE DAWSON REPORT

We find in Western industrial societies a growing interest in the regionalization of health services, an interest that is particularly accentuated in the U.S., where demands for better organization of care are increasingly loud and clear. Conferences, meetings, books and articles are appearing on — and coming out in support of — regionalization. And in this debate, an historical document — the Dawson Report[1] — is being resurrected and intensely discussed, because of its assumed paternity of the concept of regionalization. Published in Britain in 1920, the Dawson Report is generally considered to be a landmark in the history of organization and planning of health services. In fact, it is frequently presented as the definitive report on regionalization. And in the Anglo-Saxon literature, somewhat unmindful of other tongues' documents and not always aware of other countries' histories, it is presented as the *first* proposal in the world to call for regionalization of health services. For example, at a most prestigious forum — a Milbank Roundtable — that took place recently, the Dawson Report was not only credited with being the first to enunciate the concept of regionalization, but its assumed pioneering importance was given recognition through its publication as an appendix to the proceedings of the conference.[2] Usually referred to as a most foresighted document, its lack of implementation in Britain at the period of its publication is interpreted as resulting from its being too far ahead of its time. In this respect, its assumed progressivism is considered to be the cause of its doom.

Contrary to prevalent belief and in opposition to the most frequent interpretation of that report, I will try to show in the following pages of this chapter that, first, the Dawson Report was *not* the first report on regionalization in the world, and second, far from being the progressive and foresighted document that it is assumed to be, the report was, in actuality, a conservative document, produced by a Conservative-Liberal coalition as a reaction to a social movement — the socialist labour movement — that was perceived as a profound threat to the forces and constituencies that brought about and supported the report. Indeed, the lack of historical perspective that is unfortunately so characteristic of most medical care (and, I would add, sociological) literature leads authors and social analysts to consider specific events independently of and separately from the economic and political forces that historically determined them. Not surprisingly, this approach leads to conclusions that are both empirically invalid and ineffective policy-wise.

To correct this historical insensitivity, it is necessary to analyse the Dawson Report in the context of the politico-economic environment that determined it. Thus, let us go back to the period that is under discussion in this section — the beginning of the twentieth century — and try to see how and why the Dawson Report came about, i.e., what economic and political forces determined its historical emergence. But before this, a brief note to set the historical record straight. The Dawson Report was not the first report on regionalization in the world — nor even in Great Britain, for that matter. By the time the Dawson Report was published in 1920, the Zemstvo scheme, which was the first regionalized health system in the world, had been in practice since 1860 in Czarist Russia, and Dr. Semashko — a close friend of Lenin's — had produced a further report on regionalization that was implemented by the Bolsheviks after the October Revolution of 1917.[3] Ideological preferences or dislikes should not interfere — although they very frequently do — with the reporting of history.

Regarding Great Britain, the first report on regionalization was one published by the State Medical Services Association (the forerunner of the Socialist Medical Association), whose principles were supported by the majority of the labour movement at that time, and whose potentially threatening power made it necessary for the British establishment to take steps to curtail its growing influence. In essence, the Dawson Report represented the response of the British establishment to the radical programme put forward by the socialist movement and its allied State Medical Services Association (SMSA).[4] Actually, the implementation of that programme would have determined profound changes in the health sector, changes that the Dawson Report aimed to postpone and dilute. But before going further, let us elaborate on this by examining the forces that brought about the report.

The Political Determinants of the Dawson Report

As indicated in the previous pages of this volume, the first decades of the twentieth century were characterized by (1) widespread social unrest on the part of growing labour and socialist movements, considerably influenced by the Soviet Revolution of 1917, and by (2) World War I, which required great sacrifices from the working class and, indeed, from the majority of the British population — sacrifices that were extracted on the basis of the promise of a better Britain and a better world after the war. As Lloyd George, that perceptive, subtle and intelligent conservative Prime Minister of the Liberal Government, had indicated in 1917, 'The working class will be expecting a really new world. They will never go back to where they were prior to the war'.[5]

Actually, the dissatisfaction of the labour movement with its working and living conditions was determining a new level of militancy that was a threat not only to the representatives of the upper class and its political arms — the Conservative and Liberal Parties — but even to the political and Parliamentarian leadership of the Labour Party. And it was that level of militancy, heightened by the winds of social unrest sweeping all over Europe (and culminating in the Soviet Revolution of 1917), that was responsible for the emergence of the most radical Constitution and the most militant and demanding programme that the Labour Party has ever had. It was in February of 1918, several months after the Soviet Revolution, that the Labour Party, by a nearly unanimous vote, included in its Constitution the famous Clause 4 — still there today — which formally mandates the Party 'to secure for the workers by hand or by brain the full fruits of their industry and the most equitable distribution thereof that may be possible, upon the basis of the common ownership of the means of production'.[6]

In its programme for the December elections of 1918, significantly entitled *Labour and the New Social Order,* the Labour Party demanded the reconstruction of not 'this or that piece of social machinery, but of society itself', and advocated the immediate nationalization of the land, railways, mines, production of electricity, industrial insurance companies, canals, harbours, and steamship lines. The state was to assume responsibility for providing every citizen with a minimum standard of health, education, leisure and subsistence, and guarantee employment to every willing worker, 'by hand or by brain', with social services paid for by progressive taxation and administered by local authorities.[7] The programme also demanded the abolition of the House of Lords.[8]

The health branch of that movement, the State Medical Services Association, called for full state ownership of hospitals and health facilities, with the establishment of regional integrated schemes in which full-time salaried physicians and other personnel would provide both curative and preventive services, at different levels of care. On the first level, there would be 'clinical or health centres', where physicians would provide primary and community care and work in close collaboration with the secondary care centres or hospitals, with which they would share staff, laboratories, libraries, and central sterile supply. In summary, the aim was both to nationalize and to regionalize the health services, which were programmed to be under the administration of local authorities. An interesting footnote, incidentally, is that in several editorials *The Lancet*, Britain's oldest and most influential medical journal, but one noted for its radical maverick stands, supported such a programme.[9]

All in all, the Labour Party's programme in the economic and social sectors represented a clear threat to the British establishment. The political leader of this establishment, Lloyd George, finished up his closing speech in the December campaign by warning the British electorate that 'the Labour Party is being run by . . . a Bolshevik group'.[10] These were his last words in that speech and in that campaign — a campaign run by Conservatives and Liberals alike with a heavy dose of scare tactics against the supposed Bolshevik threat. The electorate did not heed the warnings, however. Quite to the contrary. It is an indication of the great receptivity to the radical programme of Labour, on the part of not only the working class, but also other sectors of the population, that the number of votes for Labour increased from 400,000 in the last election of 1910 to 2.5 million in 1918, representing 22% of the total vote and converting the Labour Party to the largest opposition party in the Parliament.[11]

Rapid growth of a party with such a radical programme for restructuring Britain was considerably disquieting to the English establishment of that time. Moreover, the popular mood after the election represented a clear threat to the system, particularly considering that the Government was not even sure it could count on the Army and Police if things got out of hand. Expressing such doubts early in 1919, the War Office had sent a secret circular to all commanding officers of troops stationed in Britain, asking — *inter alia* — whether soldiers would respond to orders to break strikes and preserve the social peace.[12] The social climate was clearly a conflictive one. And thus, the Government had to react defensively to the threat and take steps to beat back the growing influence of Labour. And that response in the health sector was the Dawson Report, published in 1920, one year after the Ministry of Health had been established. Lord Dawson, incidentally, was the first Minister of Health in Lloyd George's Government.

The Dawson Report accepted some of the principles and, indeed, even some of the terminology of the SMSA reports. But, in general, it very considerably diluted the recommendations of the socialists, and paid great attention to the interests of the medical profession, whose collaboration was considered essential for the implementation of the report. It was, in summary, the conservative rebuttal to the socialist call for regionalization.[13]

For example, wherever the initial socialist programme spoke of integration, the Dawson Report substituted co-ordination. It did not speak of integrating curative with preventive services, but rather referred to co-ordinating these two services and recommended that they continue to be provided by different types of personnel. Nor did it speak of integration of primary and secondary care, as the socialist proposals had, but rather set forth the co-ordination of the proposed health centre, which would be a cottage hospital (with provisions for private beds), with the secondary care centre or hospital, to be staffed by part-time consultants paid on a fee-for-service basis (with ample provision for private beds to handle their inpatient private practice as well). The report sided with the medical profession in its opposition to providing free care and a full-time salaried service, claiming that the latter 'would tend by its machinery to discourage initiative, to diminish the sense of responsibility and to encourage mediocrity'.[14] In its stead, general practitioners and consultants were to continue in private practice, leaving it up to them and to the financial ability of the patient to determine where, when, and how a patient would be seen.

Last, but certainly not least, it sided against the socialist alternative of integrating municipal and voluntary hospitals into a unified structure, supporting instead the continuation of the two systems — which reflected the two-class system of care prevalent at the time and that has been described in the previous section. The report spoke very approvingly of the voluntary system, for which it recommended all types of support — support that subsequently came in 1923 when Parliament granted £500,000 to assist the voluntary, but not municipal, hospitals.[15]

In summary, the Dawson Report represented the response of a conservative government to a progressive, and therefore threatening trend. And the fact that it was not implemented does not signify that it was ahead of its time, but rather reflects the fact that the progressive wave that determined the need to publish such a report lost its strength and was finally defeated. Thus, the need to implement the Dawson Report's recommendations diminished substantially. Indeed, the pressure that had been building up and that was reflected in the dramatic electoral gains for Labour in 1918, culminated, on 'Black Friday' of 1921, in an open confrontation between the labour movement and Lloyd George's government. In February of that year, the Lloyd George Government announced that it intended to decontrol the coal mines, which had been under state control, and restore full responsibility for their management to the owners. And the terms that the owners offered included a drastic wage reduction. The coalminers, with their other allies in the Triple Alliance — dockers and railway workers — decided to go out on a general strike beginning Friday, the 15th of April — 'Black Friday'. In response, Lloyd George announced that he was calling out the Army. Not wanting to face the possible outbreak of a civil war, the trade union leaders called off the strike, and as Miliband indicates, with that decision, the spine of the revolt was broken.[16]

Actually, not unlike other historical movements of confrontation, the leadership of the unions and the Labour Party shifted the *champ de bataille* from the streets to Parliament. Heavily influenced by Bernstein's doctrines of gradual and evolutionary change (as opposed to Lenin's strategy of revolutionary change), the Labour Party leadership had always opposed any expression of 'class war', calling instead for the collaboration and brotherhood of all men and women in their quest for social justice. As MacDonald, one of the most important figures in Labour Party history, had indicated, the leadership of the Party had always felt that 'socialism reflected the growth of society, not the uprising of a class', and that the goals of socialism were to be furthered by 'the close collaboration of all men of good will on the basis of conceptions of right and wrong common to all classes'.[17] Thus, the call by that leadership was not to class war, but to 'common sense and reason' — to be expressed primarily in Parliament.[18] The shift of conflict from the streets to Parliament had the effect, in 1921, of very strongly diluting the threat represented by a nationwide strike. Indeed, the impressive walls of Parliament were able to control and defuse the protest movement far more effectively than the Army and Police ever could have done. And in that shift, the pressure that had determined the Dawson Report disappeared.

The General Strike of 1926 and the Second Emergence of Calls for Reorganization of the Health Sector

The weakening of labour's resistance in 1921 took away the pressure that had originally prompted discussion of the reorganization of the health sector. And it was not until later, when the coalminers regrouped again and led the General Strike of 1926, that any more was said about health care, its funding and its reorganization. The origins of the General Strike lie in a financial crisis faced by the coal industry in 1925. For both the coal owners and the Government, the solution was a clear one — further substantial reduction of the coal miners' wages. On 29 July, the Prime Minister had told the coalmine owners that the Government would not come to the aid of the industry, and that the coal industry must stand on its own economic foundation. Moreover, he added, 'all the workers of this country have got to take reductions in wages to help put industry on its feet'.[19] This, then, was the genesis of the General Strike. The coalminers and the Trades Union Congress called a nationwide work stoppage. And the Government yielded on 31 July 1925 ('Red Friday', as it was jubilantly called by the labour movement), providing for a subsidy until 1 May 1926, at which time a Royal Commission was to make further recommendations.[20] Large sectors of the labour movement interpreted this move as a delaying tactic, which would allow the Government and the coalmine owners time to get organized.[21]

Moreover, the composition of the Royal Commission, with its great predominance of bankers and corporate owners, including Sir

William Beveridge of later fame, was hardly reassuring. Beveridge, an economist and financier, had been a leading writer for the *Morning Post*, whose proprietor was the pro-fascist, coalmine-owning Duke of Northumberland.[22] And the recommendations of this Commission confirmed these reservations. Included among them was the recommendation that miners' wages be cut or, alternatively, that working hours be lengthened. Large sectors of the mine owners accepted this proposal. The Miners' Federation rejected it, but requested further consultations with the Government and coalmine owners.[23]

On 30 April, the King signed a State of Emergency into effect, moving troops into South Wales and Scotland (the mining regions). The next morning, 1st May, the Trades Union Congress voted, by an overwhelming majority, to go out on a national strike, with stoppages in all the main sectors of economic life, except for sanitary and health services.[24] The Prime Minister, Lord Baldwin, indicated that 'the general strike was not a strike but an attempted revolution'.[25] And he called on all 'reasonable and responsible people' to rally round the Government in its confrontation with the unions — which the 'reasonable people' did.[26] Cardinal Bourne warned that to strike was 'to sin against the obedience which we owe to God',[27] and the British Broadcasting Corporation's General Manager, John Reith, explicitly stated that the BBC should serve the Government, and therefore sided against the strikers and refused to allow labour leaders to expose their views over that medium.[28]

All governmental resources were mobilized to break the strike — from the Army and the Navy to Winston Churchill. Churchill, the voice of the heavy-handed conservative wing of the establishment, had previously warned that socialism was worse than war,[29] and asked for the use of tanks to crush the strikers.[30] Also, the Government ordered hospitals to stop all assistance and delivery of food and services to strikers and their dependents. And the Houses of Parliament passed an act empowering the Ministry of Health to 'suspend the Board of Guardians who refused the Minister's instructions to stop relief and the supply of free meals for the children of the destitute'.[31]

This tough stand was accompanied by calls from the Prime Minister to the working class to be reasonable because, as the Minister insisted, he was 'capable of and sensitive to justice'. Indeed, the brute force of the stick had to be accompanied by the promise of the carrot.

It was in this atmosphere and, some may convincingly add, with this intent, that the 1926 Royal Commission on National Health Insurance made its report,[32] advising an increase in coverage to include workers' dependents and an expansion of benefits to increase specialized services. Two members of the Commission even called for a major reorganization of the health services, with funding to come from general revenues.

But, as in 1921, the Conservative–Liberal establishment's call to arms (i.e., the Army) again intimidated the Labour leadership. The Labour Party backed down and, once more, channelled protest into the halls of Parliament. The moderates, including Beatrice Webb — who had all along opposed the General Strike, to the point of coming out against sending relief to the strikers — took over the leadership of the Party[33] and tried to revitalize the Parliamentarian strategy, whose credibility had been seriously damaged prior to and during the strike. But, as in 1921, the defeat of the 1926 General Strike and the subsequent breakdown of the labour movement once again removed the social pressure that could have determined the need to enact further social reform. The recommendations of the Royal Commission were never accepted, let alone implemented. And it was not until the late 1930's that health and medical terminology reappeared in legislative proposals.

NOTES

1 Consultative Council on Medical and Allied Services, *Interim Report on the Future Position of Medical and Allied Services*, London, Her Majesty's Stationery Office (1920).

2 'Proceedings' reprinted in E. W. Saward (ed.), *The Regionalization of Personal Health Services*, London, Prodist (1975).

3 See H. Sigerist, *Medicine and Health in the Soviet Union*, New York, Citadel Press (1947). Also 'Zemstvo Medicine and / or the World's First Attempt to Regionalize Medicine', in V. Navarro, *Social Security and Medicine in the USSR. A Marxist Critique*, Lexington, Mass., Lexington Books / D.C. Heath (1977).

4 D.S. Murray, *Why a National Health Service? The Part Played by the Socialist Medical Association*, London, Pemberton Books (1971).

5 Mentioned in 'Labour and the Old Social Order', in R. Miliband, *Parliamentary Socialism*, London, Merlin Press (1973), pp. 59-65.

6 In 1929, this clause was expanded to include 'the means of distribution and exchange and the best obtainable system of popular administration and control of each industry and service'.

7 For a full account and discussion of the Labour Party programme and its consequences, see Miliband, *op. cit.*, pp. 60-63.

8 *Labour Party Annual Conference Report*, January 1918, p. 136.

9 See J. Tudor Hart, 'Reform and Reaction in Medical Care', *International Journal of Health Services*, 2 (November, 1972), p. 571. Also, Murray, *op. cit.*

10 C.L. Mowat, *Britain Between the Wars, 1918-1940*, London, Methuen (1968), p. 5.

11 Miliband, *op. cit.*, p. 64

12 W.H. Crook, *The General Strike*, Chapel Hill, University of North Carolina Press (1931), pp. 240-242.

13 J. Tudor Hart. 'Reform and Reaction in Medical Care', *op. cit.*; and Murray, *op. cit.*

14 Consultative Council on Medical and Allied Services, *op. cit.*, Section III.

15 O. Anderson, *op. cit.*, p. 64.

16 Miliband, *op. cit.*, p. 87.

17 F. Bealey and H. Pelling, *Labour and Politics, 1900-1906*, London, Macmillan (1958).

18 *Ibid.*

19 R.P. Arnot, *General Strike, May 1926: Its Origin and History*, New York, Augustus M. Kelley (1967), pp. 376-377.

20 Miliband, *op. cit.*, p. 377.

21 T.J. Jones, *Lloyd George*, New York, Random House (1951), p. 217.

22 C. Farman, *May 1926, The General Strike*, London, Panther Books (1974), p. 73.

23 Trades Union Congress General Council, *The Mining Crisis and the National Strike*, London (1927), p. 61.

24 *Ibid.*, p. 33.

25 *British Gazette*, May 10, 1926, p. 1.

26 Miliband, *op. cit.*, p. 138.

27 Arnot, *op. cit.*, p. 203.

28 J.C.W. Reith, *Into the Wind*, London, Hodder & Stoughton (1949), p. 108.

29 R.W. Lyman, *The First Labour Government, 1924*, London, Chapman & Hall (1953), p. 61.

30 Miliband, *op. cit.*, p. 137.

31 *Ibid.*

32 Royal Commission on National Health Insurance, *Report*, London, Her Majesty's Stationery Office, Command Paper 2596 (1926).

33 M. Cole (ed.), *Beatrice Webb's Diaries, 1924-1932*, London, Longman, Green and Co. (1956), p. 89.

CHAPTER III

The Winds of Social Revolt: The Scenario for the Subsequent Creation of the NHS

THE SUPPOSED 'NOBLESSE OBLIGE' ATTITUDE OF THE ARISTOCRACY

Much has been written about why the National Health Service came about in Great Britain and took the form and shape that it did. As to the reasons for the creation of the NHS, an explanation that is frequently given is the *noblesse oblige* attitude of the British aristocracy towards the rest of society. Indeed, the same *noblesse oblige* that is assumed to have been behind the enactment of the National Health Insurance Act of 1911 is again supposed to be the motor force behind the creation of the NHS in 1948. Anderson, for example, writes that the British aristocracy

> entertain[ed] a philosophy of help to the poor minus the grudging and puritan methods of the emerging middle class after 1832 as revealed in the Poor Laws.[1]

Moreover, Anderson continues,

> In the case of medical care, the poorer classes were seen as needing comprehensiveness, not particular services or assistance for particular high-cost episodes. The underlying attitude was benevolence and paternalism.[2]

It is interesting to note that the attribution of social change to the *noblesse oblige* of the aristocracy is not infrequent in historical literature. And that attitude is assumed to be part of a broader collective orientation on the part of the aristocracy that explains, for example, the earlier development of the Welfare State in Great Britain than in other countries. As Professor Lipset from Harvard writes,

> the *noblesse oblige* morality inherent in aristocracy is an aspect of collectivity-orientation. Traditionally, Britain and Australia

appear to have stressed collectivity obligations more than have Canada and the United States.[3]

In the same way that I showed the inaccuracy of attributing the enactment of the Lloyd George Act of 1911 to the *noblesse oblige* of the British aristocracy, I will also try to demonstrate in the following section the falsity of using the same explanation for the creation of the NHS. Indeed, just as it is necessary to take into consideration the nature and level of the class struggle at the end of the nineteenth and beginning of the twentieth century in order to understand the origins of the Lloyd George Act, here again we have to pay attention to these factors if we are to understand the genesis of the NHS. And for this, we must return to the historical moment that we left at the end of the previous section, i.e., the late 1920's.

The Wall Street Crash, Class Struggle, and Their Implications in Medicine

The Wall Street crash of 1929 had a very powerful impact on all Western capitalist economies, signalling the beginning of the most profound depression the world has ever known. Unemployment was growing at a dramatic rate, with the number of unemployed in July of 1930 — 2,800,000 people — being the highest recorded in British history. Not unlike today's depression, calls were made, primarily by Conservatives and Liberals, to dramatically reduce public expenditures and workers' wages, so as to allow the shift of capital from the public to the private sector and to encourage private investment.[4]

As a result of this economic deterioration, the working class became increasingly militant and disillusioned with its Parliamentarian leadership, which had been — in the opinion of many — too accommodating to Conservative and Liberal policies. Powerful new voices were being raised within the labour movement on whether the Labour Party leadership's emphasis on evolution and the Parliamentarian road to power was, in fact, an appropriate strategy for Britain at that time. None other than Harold Laski, a director of the London School of Economics, was asking in 1932 whether

> evolutionary socialism [had] deceived itself in believing that it can establish itself by peaceful means within the ambit of the capitalist system.

And he added that

> the road to power is far harder than Labour has, so far, been led to imagine.[5]

And in his introduction to *Essays on Fabian Socialism*, George Bernard Shaw wrote that

> when [years past] the greatest socialist of that day, the poet and craftsman William Morris, told the workers that there was no hope for them save in revolution, we said that if that were true, there was no hope at all for them, and urged them to save themselves through Parliament, the municipalities and the franchise. It is not so certain today . . . that Morris was not right.[6]

Accompanying these calls for actual revolution were demands, emerging from the 1932 Annual Conference of the Labour Party, for a profound socialist transformation of Britain. Similar demands were made by a large majority in the 1933 Annual Conference, culminating with the electoral programme for 1934 that demanded, in a manifesto entitled 'For Socialism and Peace', the nationalization of banking, insurance, transport, and electricity. In the health sector, the Party manifesto indicated that

> (1) The nation needs a medical service planned as a whole;
>
> (2) It must be preventive as well as curative; and neither paid private doctoring nor National Health Insurance can deal adequately with the prevention of ill-health;
>
> (3) The service must be complete and it must be open to all, *so that poverty shall be no bar to health*;
>
> (4) It must be efficient and up-to-date *providing for team work* — and only the community can achieve this by a planned disposition of hospitals, doctors, etc.;
>
> (5) It must offer a *fair deal to doctor and patient* alike and only a system of *whole time, salaried and pensionable doctoring* will do.[7]

As Stark Murray points out, the scheme was to be nationally supervised, regionally planned and locally administered through linked general hospitals and health centres, with local health centres and other units extending right down to the local population.[8]

The level of militancy of the working class and the far-reaching demands put forth by Labour clearly represented, once again, a threat to the British establishment and its political arms, the Conservative and Liberal Parties. In the health sector, the socialist demands represented a serious challenge to the medical profession as well as to the voluntary hospital system. Thus, those in positions of power within the health sector had to take steps to avoid that sector's socialization. And the strategy they chose was the one so eloquently summarized in a line from Giuseppe di Lampedusa's *The Leopard*: 'If we want things to stay as they are, things will have to change . . .'.[9] Consequently, the medical profession, primarily the British Medical Association, issued the 1938 BMA Report[10] suggesting a reorganization of the British health services, and specifically recommending voluntary co-ordination among hospitals instead of integration, and the extension of the National Health Insurance to the entire working class. It is interesting, once again, to note that the 1938 BMA report on reorganization has been characterized by most social analysts as an extremely farsighted and progressive document. Anderson, for example, writes

> It is astonishing that the BMA issued as early as 1938 a program to reorganize the British health service. Hardly ever has the medical profession taken the initiative in suggesting reforms before any other important body in society, particularly the government. It has usually reacted rather than acted.[11]

But when this report is analysed politically and historically, one does not find anything astonishing about such a response. The BMA had clearly been placed on the defensive by Labour. And as any other power group would be, the BMA was intent upon diluting that threat. By advocating co-operation among hospitals, for example, it was attempting to bypass the integration sought by the socialists. And by requesting an expansion of the population coverage, as Forsyth rightly indicates, the BMA wanted to

> insure doctors against the patients' inability to pay rather than insure patients against the high cost of medical services.[12]

It was also at this time, incidentally, that the AMA in the United States was establishing Blue Shield, with similar purposes in mind.

Regarding the voluntary hospital sector, the demand by the Labour Movement to integrate both voluntary and municipal hospitals, under the administrative responsibility of the local authorities, did indeed represent a serious threat to the voluntary hospital establishment.[13] The economic depression of the 1930's was also seriously jeopardizing the survival of that system. Responding to these threats, Lord Nuffield established the Nuffield Provincial Hospitals Trust in 1939, endowing it with one million shares in Morris Motors, Ltd. As Forsyth has indicated, 'The Nuffield Provincial Hospitals Trust . . . sprang very much from a desire to save the voluntary hospital movement'.[14] And it was part and parcel of that desire that the voluntary — and municipal— system should be co-ordinated and regionalized, using direct financial incentives as the proper means of doing the stimulating.

In summary, then, the responses of the BMA and the voluntary hospital system can be attributed to the threat represented by the socialist alternative. That threat became diluted, however, and conflict was postponed, with the advent of World War II. This historical event of monumental importance triggered the creation of the Welfare State in Britain. Because of its significance, let us move on to an analysis of the state of class relations during World War II and identify some of their implications for the health sector.

NOTES

1 O. Anderson, *op. cit.*, p. 93.

2 *Ibid.*

3 Quoted in *Ibid.*, pp. 93-94.

4 Miliband, *op. cit.*, p. 169.

5 H. Laski, *The Crisis and the Constitution*, London, Hogarth Press (1932), p. 9.

6 G.B. Shaw (ed.), *Essays on Fabian Socialism*, London, Constable (1931), p. ix.

7 *Labour Party Annual Conference Report* (1934).

8 Murray, *op. cit.*

9 G. Lampedusa, *The Leopard*, New York, Random House (1960).

10 British Medical Association, *A General Medical Service for the Nation*, London, BMA (1938).

11 O. Anderson, *op. cit.*, p. 82.

12 Forsyth, *Doctors and State Medicine*, *op. cit.*, p. 15.

13 For an historical analysis of the development of hospitals in Great Britain, see B. Abel-Smith, *The Hospitals, 1800-1948*, London, Heinemann (1964).

14 Forsyth, *Doctors and State Medicine*, *op. cit.*, p. 86.

CHAPTER IV

Class Struggle, World War II and their Consequences in the Health Sector

The War for a New Society

World War II was accompanied in Great Britain by (1) continuous calls to put class antagonisms aside and adopt a policy of class collaboration, and (2) a need and demand for massive state intervention in all spheres of economic and social life. Later, in the second phase of the war, these characteristics became augmented by (3) a concern on the part of the British upper class to ensure working class support when the war ended. Each one of these characteristics affected the content and form of the different studies and reports that culminated, in 1949, in the approval of the National Health Services Act. Because of the importance of these characteristics, let me further elaborate on each.

In the first part of the war, class conflict was submerged by what was defined as the goal of national survival and the determination to win the lonely struggle against the Axis powers. All national will was aimed at these objectives. And, for these purposes, a political truce was declared between the Conservative and Labour Parties, and a coalition established. Let me underline here that the class struggle, although submerged, had not disappeared. Indeed, this pact and the subsequent coalition came about under the dominance and according to the terms of the capitalist class and its political arm, the Conservative Party. The fact that the Prime Minister was from the latter Party had more than symbolic value. It reflected a reality. And the nature of the blueprints for change reflected, as we will see later, this same reality.

A further consequence of war planning was the need for the active involvement of the state in most economic and social activities — an intervention that not only worked, but that proved to be an indispensable condition for victory. Actually, because of this intervention, and also because of the controls that it determined, many people — millions in fact — were better fed in wartime than in peacetime.[1] In the health sector, war planning meant state direction of the medical and hospital sectors through the Emergency Medical Service, with the need for (1) co-ordinating (but not integrating) all hospital facilities in Britain, and (2) distributing hospital resources — including human resources — to hospitals not previously attended.[2] The war effort required a better distribution and regionalization of emergency services to take care of war casualties. An interesting note here is that when specialists working in teaching hospitals (their members belonging, for the most part, to the upper class) went to non-teaching hospitals — both voluntary and municipal — they were shocked by the very poor conditions existing in these institutions, where most of the population was being cared for.[3] Particularly because of this shock, but more importantly because of the need to reassure the population that the war they were fighting was, in fact, one worth fighting, blueprints for change were developed — both inside and outside the health sector — to give the population hope for a better tomorrow. Needless to say, considering the unequal distribution of power among classes that existed in the War Coalition Government, as well as the policy of class collaboration that I spoke about earlier, it is not surprising that most of these blueprints, while containing large concessions to the working class, still bore the strong imprimatur of the capitalist class.

One of these blueprints was a plan for change in the health sector prepared by the BMA Medical Planning Commission. This Commission, set up by the BMA and the Royal Colleges, had seventy-three members, representing all sections of the medical profession, including a few from the Socialist Medical Association.[4] It was practically dominated, however, by representatives of the Royal Colleges. The final report and its recommendations went further than the previously discussed blueprint put forward by the BMA in 1938. It basically accepted the measures in the health sector, i.e., central planning and regionalized co-ordinated arrangements, that had been implemented during the war by the Coalition Government. It recommended their continuation after the war and their expansion to include, besides emergency services, all hospital services and newly-proposed health centres where general practitioners would practise. However, it did not support the proposals made by the Socialist Medical Association to (1) integrate the voluntary and municipal hospitals, and (2) place their administration in the hands of local authorities. Instead, the Commission supported the retention of the division between the two hospital systems and the overall administration of the voluntary hospitals by a central body — either the central government or, even better, a paragovernmental body or corporation, following the example of the BBC. In either case, the medical profession was to be well represented in the administrative structure of the system.

Regarding the funding and coverage of services, the Commission recommended the expansion of health insurance to the entire population, except the top 10%. This was the 'cream' of society and the sector from which most of the consultants — members of the Royal Colleges and the dominant force in the Commission — drew their clientele.

A last note regarding the Commission's report is that, contrary to widely-held belief,[5] the BMA did not support its final recommendations. Actually, they were not final, but initial draft recommendations, which the BMA expected to be defeated, or at least substantially modified, in the BMA Council meeting. As a result of that opposition, the Commission never met again, and the final report never appeared. Nonetheless, the initial draft was widely distributed. It was a fight between patricians — the Royal Colleges — and practitioners — the BMA — and one that the patricians won.[6]

In the second phase of the war, when national survival seemed assured and victory seemed possible, a renaissance of public expectations took place. The working class — the majority of the British population and those who had carried the burden of war — was determined that things would not revert to the pre-war situation. From this point on, the war was fought not only against the Axis powers, and against Nazism and Fascism, but also for a new world — one that would guarantee employment, welfare, security and greater opportunities for education. Actually, the entry of the U.S. into the war gave even further impetus to this popular demand. As Miliband indicates:

> For the American message during the war was the message of freedom rather than of free enterprise, of democracy and of opportunity, of the New Deal and of social equality.[7]

And that radicalization of the population deepened as the war progressed. As the late Richard Titmuss pointed out in his book, *Birth, Poverty, and Wealth* — written 'in the strutted basement of a

London house during a bomb-littered winter' — class differentials of property, wealth and privilege, as well as those of mortality, could no longer be tolerated.[8]

Thus, the spirit of war was giving birth to a spirit of rebellion against the old pre-war order. And that spirit had the British establishment deeply worried. Indeed, and as Forsyth rightly indicates, the British establishment was increasingly concerned about whether the working class was entirely satisfied with the reasons for fighting the war.[9] The Churchill Government had all along been forced to stress that things were going to be quite different after the war. And to demonstrate this, it produced the Beveridge Report, usually referred to as a most advanced piece of social legislation, which promised social security from the cradle to the grave, and called for the maintenance of full employment and the provision of a national health service for everyone.[10] Its importance as the determinant and generator of the NHS has, however, been greatly exaggerated.

Indeed, as Eckstein correctly points out, at the time that it appeared, the Coalition Government was already working on a plan for comprehensive health services which was more progressive in terms of its recommendations than the Beveridge Report.[11] Actually, the recommendations of the Beveridge Report for the medical sector, far from being as revolutionary as they are usually assumed to be, were remarkably similar to those of the Medical Planning Commission and heavily influenced by the Royal Colleges — the voice of the upper class medical establishment. The only major difference was that the report did not accept the exclusion from the national scheme of the top 10% of the British population advocated by the Commission's interim report. Otherwise, the Beveridge Report actually gave the imprimatur to the Commission's report. The patricians (the Royal Colleges) finally and definitively won over the practitioners (the BMA).

Preparations for the Post-War Period

The turning point of the war had come and victory was in sight. The glimmer of hope for a new world was in the eyes of many. Actually, that hope was far-reaching, extending all across Europe. The fight against Nazism and Fascism was going to be won, opening up all sorts of possibilities for the post-war period. Blueprints for this new world began appearing. And an important one was the White Paper on National Health Services,[12] prepared by the Churchill Government and published five months prior to the D-Day landing in Normandy.

To understand the nature of these blueprints, it is important to return to a point made earlier. That is, while a coalition of forces did exist, the dominant force in that Coalition Government was the Conservative Party. If we are aware of this, we can then better comprehend the nature of the White Paper. Actually, that document was, as indicated, remarkably similar in its recommendations to the report of the Medical Planning Commission. It reflected the Beveridge Report's recommendation that the new health service be fully comprehensive and free, financed out of general taxation and local rates. And in terms of organizational and administrative structure, it closely followed the one suggested by the Commission's interim report.[13] Because of the importance of these proposed arrangements for a subsequent understanding of the NHS, let us detail some of its specific recommendations concerning the areas of general practice and specialist hospital care.

The Proposed Changes in General Practice

The general practitioners were to work and be paid under a capitation system (as they were under the existing National Health Insurance), and be under contract to a Central Medical Board (CMB). Those practitioners who preferred working in health centres (to be managed and presided over by local authorities) and being paid by salary, however, were to have a joint contract with the CMB and the local authorities. An important point was that the CMB, to be controlled by the medical profession and primarily by the BMA, was supposed to regulate entry into practice, i.e., where one practised. The main rationale for this recommendation was to enable, through self-regulation, the better distribution of practitioners.[14] The CMB would establish which areas were overdoctored and which were underdoctored, and assign practitioners to the latter, denying entry into the former. Although both criteria and definitions were left unspecific, the principal was clear, i.e., the profession would become self-regulating in terms of geographical distribution. It is interesting to note that in a questionnaire sent by the leadership of the BMA to all physicians in Britain, of those (including general practitioners) who answered (50% response rate), the majority indicated that they were in favour of the CMB's regulatory functions, of the establishment of health centres, and of being paid on a salaried basis.[15] And, in general, these sentiments were strongest among younger physicians. According to S. Murray, 89% of the medical students polled were in favour of health centres.[16]

Representing primarily the older and more wealthy members, the leadership of the BMA, however, chose to ignore this poll and, in fact, opposed the majority of the provisions of the White Paper. In secret negotiations with the Conservatives, it came out against (1) the creation of a Central Medical Board, (2) the establishment of salaried services in the health centres, and (3) the control of health centres by local authorities. The health centres were supposed to be leased and rented by the local authorities to the practitioners who would, in turn, practise in them on a capitation basis and remain free to undertake private practice.[17] The Conservative Government accepted all these modifications. Because of these concessions, *the NHS was supposed to represent, for the general practitioners, the mere extension of the national health insurance scheme to the rest of the population.*

The Proposed Changes in Specialists' Services

The White Paper did not refer directly to specialists. The voluntary hospitals were to receive governmental funds, and in return a regulatory apparatus — to be further developed in 1944 in the Ministry of Health Report of the Inter-Departmental Committee on Medical Schools — would be established to assure the more equitable distribution of specialists. The White Paper supported the continuation of the two hospital systems — voluntary and municipal. For the latter, however, it suggested an ad hoc regional authority, to be appointed centrally, that would be responsible for the planning and administration of these hospitals. This further undermined the measure of control over health services by local authorities, who were to be left with only limited services, such as home nursing, health visiting and school health. The voluntary hospitals would continue as separate and independent entities, although it would be a condition for receiving grants that their plans be co-ordinated with those of the ad hoc regional authority.

Had these plans been accepted. it would have meant an expansion of the national health insurance scheme to the entire population, and a further weakening of the local authorities' control over the medical sector, shifting control even further from the public to the private agencies — the ad hoc regional committees — where the medical profession and members of the upper class were dominant. Not surprisingly, the Socialist Medical Association strongly opposed these recommendations. Instead, the SMA advocated completely salaried and integrated services, with general practitioners working in health centres, backed up by specialists' services provided in the NHS hospitals. And all hospitals and health centres were to be run by the local authorities. Their hope now was that the modified White Paper would not be implemented, and in its stead, the Labour Party would win the next election.

NOTES

1 Miliband, *op. cit.*, p. 273.

2 Forsyth, *Doctors and State Medicine, op. cit.*, p. 89.

3 *Ibid.*

4 Murray, *op. cit.*, p. 46. Also, Forsyth, *Doctors and State Medicine, op. cit.*, p. 15.

5 O. Anderson, *op. cit.*, p. 86, for example, relates that another 'astonishing' example of the British medical profession's foresight was its support for the Commission's recommendations.

6 Murray, *op. cit.*, p. 48.

7 Miliband, *op. cit.*, p. 273.

8 R.M. Titmuss, *Birth, Poverty and Wealth*, London, Hamilton Medical Books (1943), p. 9.

9 Forsyth, *Doctors and State Medicine, op. cit.*, p. 16.

10 W. Beveridge, *Report on Social Insurance and Allied Services*, London, Her Majesty's Stationery Office (1942).

11 H. Eckstein, *The English Health Service: Its Origins, Structure and Achievement*, Cambridge, Harvard University Press (1959).

12 Ministry of Health, *A National Health Service,* London, Her Majesty's Stationery Office, Command Paper 6502 (1944).

13 Forsyth, *Doctors and State Medicine, op. cit.,* p. 17.

14 *Ibid.,* pp. 16-17. Also, Willcocks, *op. cit.,* p. 27; and O. Anderson, *op. cit.,* p. 88.

15 Eckstein, *op. cit.,* p. 148.

16 Murray, *op. cit.,* p. 68.

17 Forsyth, *Doctors and State Medicine, op. cit.,* p. 19.

CHAPTER V

The Coming of Labour to Power

THE LABOUR VICTORY AND THE LABOUR PARTY PROGRAMME

The end of the war brought about a revival of class antagonisms and powerful voices in the labour movement began demanding profound changes in British society. Harold Laski, by now the Chairman of the Labour Party, ended the Party's 1945 Annual Conference with a call for a clear choice in the upcoming General Election

> between private enterprise now expressed as monopoly capitalism, and socialism that realizes that the new age is born and that only through the establishment of a Socialist Commonwealth can we realize the purposes for which we have been fighting this war.[1]

Thus, the election became an arena for a battle between two competing forces — socialism and capitalism. And the continuous call for socialism, along with the increased radicalization of the Labour Party — although not of its parliamentarian branch — was a source of grave concern to the Conservatives. They feared that the Labour Parliamentarians would no longer be able to control the labour movement, as they had so well done in the past. Actually, as Miliband points out, they increasingly viewed Laski as the Lenin of Britain, and Attlee as its Kerensky.[2] The radicalization of the population and its demand for change were clearly reflected in the results of the 1945 General Election. The Conservatives lost 172 seats and, by 142 seats, Labour won a dramatic majority. The Labour Party had become — in theory, at least — the master of Parliament and, along with its Parliamentarian representatives, had indeed been given a strong mandate for change. It is in light of this mandate — the strongest the Labour Party ever had — that it is remarkable that the programme put forward by the Labour Government was so moderate and cautious. As *The Economist* wrote in November of 1945, after publication of the Government proposals,

> an avowedly Socialist Government, with a clear Parliamentarian majority, might well have been expected to go several steps further.

> . . . If there is to be a Labour Government, the programme now stated is the least it could do without violating its election pledges.[3]

Let us analyse, for example, the nationalization policies of that Government and the industrial relations it proposed for the nationalized sectors. Regarding the former, the Government planned to nationalize those industries — coal, steel, iron, electricity, and the Bank of England — where, for the most part, there existed a consensus with the Conservatives that they should be nationalized.[4] The only exceptions to that consensus were steel and iron. As Attlee indicated, aside from the strong feelings surrounding iron and steel, 'there was not much real opposition to our nationalization proposals'.[5] The only issues of real concern were compensation and control. And arrangements for both proved to be completely satisfactory to the Conservative forces. In fact, Labour's policies regarding compensation led the American conservative, R. Brady, to conclude:

> State ownership had not altered the general structure of ownership of securities or of income plans of the community's real resources, except, possibly, somewhat to improve the status of the rentier.[6]

As for control, in those industries that were nationalized, the Government put aside the demand for workers' control and, in its stead, appointed to their governing boards men who had been members of the managerial and ownership classes of the former private industries. The Labour Government did not, as Coates rightly indicates, use its nationalization measures to shift class power within industry.[7] And the NHS was no exception to this. Actually, as I will show in the following pages, the Labour Government's policies strengthened rather than weakened the class divisions and hierarchies within the NHS — divisions which determined, incidentally, the overall composition and distribution of resources in the health sector in Britain.

Bevan, Labour and the NHS

In March of 1946, nine months after taking office, the Labour Government published the National Health Services Bill. And although the bill was very similar to the plans discussed in previous sections, nevertheless important differences did exist. An example of these differences — and one which created much resistance from the professions — was that this bill spoke of general practitioners as working primarily in health centres provided by local authorities. And in terms of the system of payment, no specific arrangement was set forth, although the BMA feared the worst, i.e., that, once the bill was approved by Parliament, the Labour Government would regulate in favour of salary. Also, the bill proposed the establishment of ad hoc professional bodies — Local Executive Councils — in charge of providing general practice services for areas analogous to those of the local authorities. Moreover, new general practitioners, as well as those changing location, would have to apply to a national Medical Practices Committee — similar to the Central Medical Board suggested by the White Paper — for permission to practise. This would provide for the self-regulatory mechanism in terms of distribution of general practitioners.[8] Not surprisingly, the BMA strongly opposed the bill.

Moreover, the idea of ad hoc regional committees that would regulate the hospital sector was abandoned in the National Health Services Bill, which favoured instead creation of regional committees, composed of several local authorities, which would co-ordinate planning for both voluntary and municipal hospitals. Thus, while not integrating these two systems — as the Socialist Medical Association was asking — the bill still gave the local authorities the responsibility for planning both services.[9] The specialists, through the Royal Colleges, expressed strong reservations to Bevan — Labour's Minister of Health — about the advisability of such an arrangement.[10]

The commitment of the Labour Government to (1) salary, (2) health centres, and (3) administration of regional committees by local authorities, was not, however, a very strong one. Indeed, the BMA's fears of being forced into a salary system were unfounded. An amendment was passed in Parliament, with Bevan's support, that had the practical effect of banning recommendation of salary.[11] And due to the opposition both of the BMA and, most importantly for Bevan, of the Royal Colleges, the idea of local authorities running the hospital sector and the health centres was quickly abandoned in favour of regional ad hoc hospital authorities.[12] Consequently, the SMA accused Bevan of betrayal. Actually, Bevan followed in the health sector the same strategy used by the Labour Government in other nationalized industries. It involved buying off the centres of opposition by granting them many privileges (the equivalent policies of compensation that Brady discussed[13]) and assuring them a dominant influence over the policies of the nationalized industries. Since these two policies, (1) granting special privileges to the medical profession in order to gain its support, and (2) allowing that profession dominance over the decision-making machinery of the NHS, are of central importance in explaining the present priorities, composition and distribution of medical resources, let us now focus on how they came about and with what consequences.

But prior to this, it is helpful to reiterate a point that was made earlier: within the medical profession, we have identified two types and two hierarchies of physicians. The top echelon of physicians included the consultants, working, for the most part, in private practice and in the voluntary hospital system, and represented by the Royal Colleges. As indicated earlier, these consultants were members of the British top establishment, both in terms of their class origin and their class position. They were the ones, as we shall see, with whom Bevan allied himself and who had a dominant voice in the shaping of the NHS. The other group was made up of the general practitioners, individualistic, middle class physicians, working in rather poor ancillary conditions and represented by the BMA. Let me further clarify that even in the BMA, the leadership spoke primarily for the interests of the older and wealthier sector of the general practitioners community. With this note, let us continue our discussion of Labour's strategy for nationalization, specifically in the health sector.

The Awarding of Class and Professional Privileges

Bevan is quoted as claiming that he 'choked [the consultants'] mouths with gold'.[14] And this indeed he did. He established a system of financial rewards that replicated the hierarchical order existing within the medical profession, in which the private consultant was at the top and the general practitioner at the bottom. Indeed, the salary which the consultants were to receive was to be complemented —

and handsomely at that — by a system of awards administered by a secret group of private consultants. Even today, the administration of this tax-funded system remains completely unaccountable to public authorities and, since it is thought that it would create 'jealousness and invidious comparisons', no annual report of grants is even published.[15] And in both the payment of salaries and the secret granting of these awards, consultants working in private practice were and are favoured.[16] Actually, to this day, in the determination of salaries, 'there is an additional weighting factor which favours specialists who work for the NHS less than half a week'.[17] Consequently, most consultants work for the NHS on only a part-time basis — a pattern reflected in the fact that in 1964, for example, 69% of them were in private practice — and their incomes are thus far higher than those of consultants working full-time for the NHS. Further contributing to this inequity of rewards in salaries is the awards system, controlled, as I have indicated, by private consultants working for the most part in teaching hospitals. According to this secret system, special awards are given every year and can be grouped into A (the best paying), B and C categories. Once given, the consultant has that annual award and its financial reward for life. A review of those receiving these awards shows that this system reinforces the teaching hospital-oriented practice, with those maintaining a private practice comprising a large majority of the recipients.[18] Altogether, salary and awards place private consultants working in teaching institutions among the best paid professionals in Britain, earning more than even the Secretary of the Treasury. Actually, not only the professional, but also the class nature of these awards clearly appears in the avowed purpose of the award system, which is

> to assure a practical and imaginative way of securing a reasonable differentiation of income and providing relatively high earnings for the significant minority.[19]

And by minority is meant primarily the upper class private consultants.

Needless to say, the other branches of the medical profession also benefited considerably from the NHS. The incomes of both general practitioners and consultants improved very dramatically as a result of the NHS. And that benefit was guaranteed by Bevan to be a stable one — a foolproof anti-inflationary system. Indeed, Bevan had indicated that it would do no harm to be generous to a few people.[20] The level of benefits, however, varied quite significantly, with a concomitant variation from the top to the bottom of the ladder in the medical profession. The class-conscious Royal Colleges made quite sure that there would not be equality within the system of rewards to the different branches of medicine. Their representative, Lord Moran — a close health advisor to Bevan — had responded to a suggestion of equalizing income between consultants and general practitioners in the following manner:

> I say emphatically no. Could anything be more absurd? . . . How can you say that the people who get to the top of the ladder are the same as the people who fall off it? It seems to me so ludicrous.[21]

In summary, then, Bevan neither questioned nor challenged the hierarchical structure of the medical sector that faithfully reproduced the overall class structure in Great Britain. As the Labour Government had done in other sectors of nationalized industry, it bought the collaboration of owners and managers of skills and property by crossing their palms with gold. And the amount of this gold depended on their class as well as their professional position within British society and within the NHS specifically.

Bevan's strategy was to count on class alliances, using the upper class within the medical profession as the point of leverage for change. There was an affinity in terms of class policies among those in power, and a shared belief that it was only 'natural' that some had more than others. Indeed while the BMA

> . . . held bitter protest meetings against certain provisions in the Bill . . . the Royal Colleges gave impressive and apparently cordial dinners for members of the government. Their aristocratic lineage held firm; at times their links with the Royal Family appeared stronger than those with their brothers in general practice . . . The Princess Royal invited the Royal College of Surgeons, of which she was an honorary Fellow, to look at their plans for rebuilding, in the months in which the Bill was laid before Parliament . . . [and] the Queen graciously accepted the office of Patron of the Royal College of Obstetricians and Gynaecologists. That same month (June 1946), the Labour Prime Minister, a Hunterian trustee, attended a dinner at the Royal College of Surgeons. Other examples can be enumerated of the interplay of the Royal Colleges with the social establishment of England.[22]

Within this reality of class unity, it would be erroneous to consider Bevan's reliance on the consultants as his allies for change within the medical sector as resulting from better use of tact or the employment of more effective strategies on the part of the leaders of the consultants, i.e., to assume that they were more astute, intelligent and polished than the BMA. Indeed their power, the Royal Colleges' power, came not from their diplomacy or tact, but primarily from their class composition and position within the class-structured society that neither the Labour Government nor Bevan intended to break or even modify. The pattern of class and professional assurances given by Bevan to the consultants clearly illustrates this.

Reassurances in the Nationalized Industries: Class and Professional Control of the NHS

In the development of the NHS legislation, Bevan followed, for the most part, the already accepted policies instituted by previous governments. There was one substantial difference, however, which is that Bevan nationalized the voluntary hospital system — a decision that could have given him the opportunity to integrate the hospital system, thereby fulfilling the long-standing demand of the Socialist Medical Association. Why did Bevan choose to nationalize the voluntary hospitals? According to his close associates, he did it to ensure the survival of these hospitals, deeply in trouble because of their large debts. Also, he was concerned that specialists would not work in these hospitals unless they were well paid and given good facilities. Indeed, according to Barbara Castle, a close associate of Bevan's,

> Nye [Bevan] asked Lord Moran (the President of the Royal College of Physicians, and whom the BMA dubbed Corkscrew Charlie because of the remarkable alliance he struck up with Nye) how he would attract first rate consultants into the peripheral provincial hospitals. When Moran replied that consultants would go there if they got an interesting job and if their financial future were secured by a proper salary, Nye paused and then said, 'Only the State could pay those salaries. This would mean the nationalization of hospitals'. And nationalize them he did.[23]

And in that nationalization, Bevan counted on the collaboration of both the Royal Colleges and the hospitals themselves. No significant opposition developed to what one irate member of the BMA called 'the largest seizure of property since Henry VIII confiscated the monasteries'.[24] Actually, in no small degree, that lack of opposition resulted from the class and professional reassurances given by Bevan to the medical profession in general, but particularly to the consultants.

This pattern of reassurance took place through many mechanisms, but most importantly through promises to the consultants of (1) priority in the system of rewards, maintaining the distinctions in the medical profession referred to in the previous section; (2) practical control over the apparatus of production of human health resources; (3) the possibility of having private beds and private practices, using the NHS facilities and services as a supplement to this; (4) a heavy influence, tantamount to control, over the main decision-making bodies of the NHS; and (5) a pattern of class dominance and professional influence over the main administrative bodies of the NHS.

The second of these reassurances meant that Bevan missed the opportunity to regionalize and to integrate the entire hospital sector. Indeed, by conceding to the Royal Colleges' desire to take the teaching hospitals out of the regionalized system and, instead, deal directly — via their Board of Governors — with the Ministry, he seriously limited the desired regionalization. As the SMA indicated, as a result of Bevan's courting the support of the Royal Colleges, the chances for regionalization and integration were thus lost. Moreover, the Royal Colleges were given a practical monopoly of control over the number and types of human resources produced in the NHS. Even today, and as we will see in Part III, this Medical Establishment retains dominance over all types of education of medical and other personnel in the NHS.

Regarding the third assurance, Bevan responded affirmatively to the consultants' demand of allowing private practice in the nationalized hospitals. Private beds still are very much a part of the NHS scene, a practice which, as was shown earlier, is actually encouraged.

As to the fourth assurance, Bevan modified the initial bill, shifting the pattern of control of the hospitals from the local authorities to ad hoc committees or regional boards. Indeed, consultants, involved in private practice for the most part, were provided with generous representation on these boards, from which other types of health personnel were practically excluded.[25]

And lastly, the clearly upper class composition of these boards reassured the consultants that no 'wild' or threatening decisions would be made by them. Indeed, here again, the nature of Labour's policies towards nationalized industry appeared quite clearly. Dismissing any form of workers' control in the nationalized hospitals, Bevan appointed individuals to their boards whom he considered to have 'the public interest at heart', 'responsible' individuals who would know how to plan and administer the medical institutions. As Anderson approvingly indicates, their appointment was based on:

> the traditional and worthy political theory . . . that reasonable citizens who are assumed to have the public interest at heart can be a buffer between the state and the rank and file citizens for whom the Service is designed.[26]

Continuing his discussion of the appointed members of these boards, Anderson remarks that it is not surprising that 'in the course of events, naturally, these citizens and professionals come from the upper social and economic classes'.[27] The fact that (1) the overwhelming majority of appointed individuals were members of the upper class and very few were members of the working class — the Labour Party's primary constituency — and (2) aside from consultants, no other health professionals or workers were appointed to these boards, exposes the clear class bias implicit in Labour's conception (and Anderson's interpretation) of 'the public interest'. A Conservative Government could not have done better.

It is interesting to note that many interpreted this upper class control of the health institutions as representing, once again, *noblesse oblige*, i.e., the altruistically-motivated carrying of the 'burden' of leading society. Anderson, for example, attributes this control to 'a continuation of the upper class *noblesse oblige* atmosphere of the governing boards'.[28] I question, however, as indicated earlier, the presence of such noble motivation. Representatives of the upper class were on these boards as part and parcel of a clear Labour policy designed to reassure both the capitalist class and its component in the health sector — the consultants — that the revolutionary changes they so feared would not take place. It was never Labour's intention, either inside or outside the health sector, to shift the existent pattern of class control in British society.

WAS THE 1948 NHS ACT A REVOLUTIONARY STEP?

According to the majority of authors and analysts, the NHS Act was a most revolutionary step, opening the way to what is considered to be the most significant piece of social engineering in the Western world. But I question such hyperbole in judgement. While agreeing that it represented a very positive victory for the working class, I would maintain that the implementation of that Act was far from the revolutionary advance that it is generally assumed to have been.

Indeed, the level of the class struggle after World War II, described above, indicates that the working class was ready for and demanding far more change than the Labour leadership envisioned. As Murray writes

> In the atmosphere of 1946 when people were ready for great new moves, it was strange that Bevan, the Labour Minister of Health, did not see and did not grasp the opportunity to break with the past.[29]

Yet considering the overall history and performance of the Labour Party, Labour's lack of receptivity to the demand for profound change seems hardly surprising. It was, in fact, its trademark.

In summary, then, the NHS represented an expansion of the National Health Insurance to the entire population — not a minor step in itself — but in light of the mood for change in 1946, hardly a revolutionary one. General practitioners continued practising in the same setting as before, and retained the much-desired autonomy which, in the long run, has very seriously hurt general practice in Britain. General practice was then, as it remains today, the great 'Cinderella' of the NHS. As we will discuss later, the percentage of the NHS budget going towards general practice has declined very dramatically. Within the medical profession those who have benefited most have been the consultants, who made substantial gains, both in income and power, with the implementation of the NHS Act. They, the patricians, implanted themselves on the NHS apparatus, heavily influencing the pattern of distribution and composition of resources within the NHS. And it is that pattern of dominance that explains, as I will show later, many of the attributed weaknesses of the present NHS, including its strong hospital orientation, the emigration of many of its physicians, and long waiting lists for its patients, among others. Indeed, as we will see in Part III, it is precisely that pattern of class and professional dominance which is primarily responsible for the present situation of the NHS. And it was in 1971, close to twenty-five years after the creation of the NHS, that none other than Crossman — the Secretary of State for Social Services between 1968 and 1970 — reflected on this pattern of class and professional control over main organs of the NHS, such as the Regional Hospital Boards, and stated,

> The RHB is the most perfect example of self-perpetuating oligarchy since the Persians' rule by Satraps . . . Consultants are the most powerful autocrats in the world to order about chairmen of Regional Hospital Boards. A real iron law of oligarchy with the minister appointing the RHB and the consultants appointing themselves. . . . What chance is there of a shift of money to the community services or long-stay hospitals? They've the same vested interest; I mean the consultants. They are the most ruthlessly egotistical administrators I have ever met in my life. They know nothing of what goes on outside the hospitals and resent having to visit them. These vast new palaces are justified for the convenience of the consultants. It is a marvellous health service for those that are excitingly ill, not desperately ill — you mustn't die boringly for the consultants . . . [in putting forward the new proposals] I was told there would be friction at the top. I said 'Thank God' — a strong Elephant and Castle with a Minister giving the directives — strong areas with local representatives — and weak regions for certain services that must be organized regionally. . . . [In my visits around the country] the major complaint was 'managerial bossdom.'[30]

It was the pattern of class and professional alliances that Labour established in the creation of the NHS that determined the subsequent set of class and professional dominances in the NHS. And those policies of class and professional conviviality were replicated, once again, in the 1974 reorganization of the NHS.

NOTES

1 *Labour Party Annual Conference Report* (1945), p. 108.

2 Miliband, *op. cit.*, p. 284.

3 *The Economist* (November, 1945).

4 R.A. Brady, *Crisis in Britain: Plans and Achievements of the Labour Government*, London, Cambridge University Press (1950), p. 41.

5 C.R. Attlee, *As It Happened*, London, W. Heinemann (1954), p. 165.

6 Brady, *op. cit.*, p. 509.

7 'The Labour Governments of 1945-51', in D. Coates, *The Labour Party and the Struggle for Socialism,* London, Cambridge University Press (1975), p. 58.

8 Willcocks, *op. cit.*, p. 83.

9 Forsyth, *Doctors and State Medicine, op. cit.,* p. 92.

10 *Ibid.*

11 Willcocks, *op. cit.,* p. 83.

12 Murray, *op. cit.,*

13 Brady, *op. cit.*

14 J. Tudor Hart, 'Bevan and the Doctors', *The Lancet,* ii(7839) (1973), p. 1196.

15 Royal Commission on Doctors' and Dentists' Remuneration, *Report to Parliament, February, 1960,* London, Her Majesty's Stationery Office, Command Paper 939 (1960).

16 Forsyth, *Doctors and State Medicine, op. cit.,* p. 29.

17 *Ibid.*

18 Forsyth, *Doctors and State Medicine, op. cit.,* p. 32; and J. Robson, 'The NHS Company, Inc.? The Social Consequence of the Professional Dominance in the National Health Service', *International Journal of Health Services,* 3(3) (Summer, 1973), pp. 413-426.

19 Royal Commission on Doctors' and Dentists' Remuneration, *op. cit.,* p. 81.

20 Forsyth, *Doctors and State Medicine, op. cit.*

21 Quoted in *Ibid.,* p. 31.

22 R. Stevens, *Medical Practice in Modern England: The Impact of Specialization and State Medicine,* New Haven, Yale University Press (1966) pp. 77-78.

23 B. Castle, *NHS Revisited,* London, Fabian Society (Tract No. 440) (1976), p. 4.

24 *Ibid.*

25 Murray, *op. cit.,* p. 83.

26 O. Anderson, *op. cit.,* p. 92.

27 *Ibid.,* p. 92.

28 *Ibid.*

29 Murray, *op. cit.*

30 Quoted in A. Learmonth, *Health,* London, Open University Press (1972), p. 88.

CHAPTER VI

The 1974 Reorganization of the NHS

THE POLITICAL DETERMINANTS OF THE REORGANIZATION

On 5 July 1973, the same month in which, twenty-five years earlier, the NHS began, the British Government was given approval to implement the National Health Service Reorganization Bill, and thus to restructure the NHS.[1] Many articles, documents and reports have been written, both prior to and after that date, concerning the main features of this reorganization.[2] Very few references, however, deal with the question of why this reorganization took place at the time it did, and took the particular form that it did. Actually, the few references that do touch on these questions tend to explain the timing and configuration of these reforms in terms of political forces within the health sector itself. In other words, it is frequently assumed that forces *within* the NHS — specifically that sector's dominant groups — determined the timing and form of its reorganization. And a series of reports, commissions and studies, prepared by various medical groups and élites who were demanding such restructuring, are then presented as supportive evidence for this assumption that the 1974 reorganization resulted from pressures that had been building up within the health sector for better co-ordination and integration of the three branches of the NHS — the supposed aim of the 1974 reorganization.[3]

I question both these assumptions, i.e., that the 1974 reorganization was primarily motivated by pressures from within the health sector, and that its primary aim was that of achieving better co-ordination and integration of the three branches of the NHS. Indeed, I believe that the primary determinants of that reorganization were political and economic forces from *outside*, not within, the health sector — forces, incidentally, which were intertwined with and related to the particular state of the class forces in the Britain of the 1950's and 60's. It was, then, the concretization and level of the conflict between those forces which determined the timing, shape and objectives of the 1974 reorganization. Let me elaborate on this by resuming the analysis of class forces in Britain at the time we left it in the previous section, i.e., after the implementation of the National Health Service.

The Political Forces in the 1950's and 60's in Britain

The defeat of the Labour Party in 1951 was perceived by many within that Party's leadership as an opportunity for rethinking Labour's strategy for the 1950's. Many felt confident that the implementation of Conservative policies — including denationalization in general, and curtailment of the NHS in particular — would discredit that Party and bring Labour back into power in the approaching elections. The Conservatives, however, did not act according to Labour's expectations. They continued to follow, for the most part, the policies and programmes initiated by Labour. Moreover, fears that the Conservatives would dismantle the NHS proved to be unfounded.

Furthermore, the defeat of Labour in the 1951 elections and what was perceived to be Labour's lack of election appeal strengthened the hand of the moderate wing of that Party, which called for the dilution of those past demands which they claimed the electorate may have considered too radical. Thus, there followed a continuous series of retreats from past commitments, and a desire on the part of Labour for what Miliband defines as middle class respectability and acceptability.[4]

It was the era of the triumph of Gaitskell and the influence of Crosland. It was, indeed, the intention of Labour to shed its class character and become attractive to the middle class and *petite bourgeoisie*. Its appeal was to be not only to the working class, but, as Gaitskell described it, to those 'ordinary decent people who do not probably think a great deal about politics'.[5] Indeed, the leadership now resented that class identification, stressing that, contrary to what the Conservatives accused Labour of being, the Party was a 'far better cross-section of the community than the Tories, who are still overwhelmingly drawn from a single social class'.[6]

Also, and as part of this 'new look', the Party programme de-emphasized nationalization, which, in the words of the moderates' main theoretician — Crosland — had become largely 'irrelevant'.[7]

Except for steel and roads, where the Party continued to demand nationalization, nationalization for the rest of the economy was considered as justifiable only in those sectors and industries where productivity was seriously lacking. A strong movement — and one which did not succeed — emerged within the leadership of the Party, with the intent of eliminating from the Party's Constitution the famous Clause 4, which committed Labour then — as it does today — to the nationalization of the means of production.[8] The result of these changes was that in the eyes of the electorate the two parties started to look more and more alike. Actually, according to a 1959 Gallup Poll, the percentage of the population which did not recognize any difference between the two parties had grown to nearly 40%.[9] And the Labour Party leadership's main claim in the 1959 election was that they were the party of efficiency, the party that could best manage the capitalist economy.[10] Similarly, in the following election of 1964, it was no longer a new Britain that was promised, but rather, a more efficient and compassionate management of the old order.[11] Thus, when Labour won power (by a small margin in 1964, and then by a larger margin in 1966), nationalization was relegated to a very low position on the Party's agenda.[12] In its stead, it proposed (1) a major reorganization of industry, so as to stimulate its productivity and efficiency; (2) the development of a planning apparatus; (3) a reorganization of the public administration; and (4) a reorganization of the public services, including the NHS. It was Labour's intention to save and indeed strengthen the ailing British capitalist economy, by stimulating the private sector and rationalizing the public one. This aim was further reinforced when in 1967, due to the dramatic balance of payments, the pound had to be devalued. It had been the policy of that Government — under the influence of Callaghan — then Minister of the Treasury and, later, Britain's Prime Minister — to consider as its first objective the saving of the pound. But it failed to do so.[13] This failure brought about an even stronger commitment by the Labour Government in 1967 to the reorganization of industry, with a wide and generous programme of assistance to the private sector, as well as rationalization of the public one.

The Labour Government's response to the economic crises of the 1960's included a number of specific measures. First, there were dramatic cuts in public expenditure, including expenditures on health services, education and housing, with the discontinuation of the provision of free milk to pupils of secondary schools.[14]

Second, grants were provided to industry in order to stimulate private investment. And the extra state revenues were to come not from increased taxation of personal income, but from an increase in direct and indirect charges on goods and services. Part of this policy was the re-introduction of prescription charges and an increase in dental fees. Needless to say, these policies hurt the working class far more than they did the upper class.

Third, steps were taken to reorganize the public administration so that it would become more efficient and productive. And this call for better public administration also stimulated a parallel demand for a higher degree of centralization of that administration. It was assumed that the latter would lead to the former. An example of these policies in the health sector was the centralization of the central government's responsibilities for medical care and the national insurance scheme into one office — that of the Secretary of the Department of Health and Social Security (DHSS). This centralization of policy, along with the amalgamation of the Ministries of Health and Social Security into DHSS, was part of an overall strategy of bringing large areas of policy together under a single cabinet minister.[15] That centralization was further accentuated in 1971, with the integration of the Children's Department of the Home Office into the DHSS.

Fourth, and as part of this call for better and more efficient administration, a reorganization of local government and social services, including the NHS, was proposed. In both cases, the aim was to strengthen the centralization of policy and the elements of management within both the local government and the social services sector. Thus, several Royal Commissions appeared in different sectors, aimed at more efficient and less costly management of public resources. One of these was the Royal Commission on Local Government, which advocated an expanded type of local authority, with broader management responsibilities than before.[16] Similar calls for administrative reform appeared in the health sector. Specifically in terms of the NHS, the enormous increase in expenditures in the health sector — from 455 million pounds to approximately 2,500 million pounds within 25 years — had created a good deal of alarm, leading to a demand for slowing down, cutting back, and generally trimming the fat in the NHS. And it was this concern that produced the call for further strengthening the centralized direction of the NHS and its mangement structure, as well as an exploration of alternatives to the care provided by costly hospital-oriented medicine. Demands for centralization led in turn to the series of Green Papers and related documents that culminated in the 1974 reorganization. And the second set of demands, concerning the exploration of alternatives to hospital-oriented medicine, determined the initial steps taken to strengthen general practice services. As they are important, I will go into these policies in greater detail.

Basic Documents Preceding the 1974 Reorganization: The Difference Between the Labour and Conservative Strategies

The first and second Green Papers,[17,18] put out by the Labour Governments of 1968 and 1970 respectively, were aimed at breaking with what was defined as a pattern of intolerable duplication, waste, and lack of co-ordination through strengthening the co-ordination of the three branches of the NHS. Actually, the first Green Paper went so far as to speak of integration of these three branches into Area Health Authorities which would be responsible for the combined planning and administration of the three branches. However, what was perceived as a need for central planning by the central government was seriously complicated by the existence of 625 separate bodies responsible for the planning and / or administration of different — and, on occasions, the same — services.[19] The solution to this wastage, duplication and lack of co-ordination was considered to be the total merger of hospital and community services, under the jurisdiction of ninety Area Health Authorities, which were to be ad hoc bodies directly accountable to the central government. They — the AHAs — would have the same boundaries as the local authorities.

Let me underline that, although similar in their aims and recommendations, the two Labour Green Papers had some meaningful differences. And one was that, while the first Green Paper deliberately excluded the regional tier and proposed direct accountability of the area authority to the central government, the second spoke of a Regional Health Council (RHC), also appointed by the central government, which would have planning and advisory — but not executive — responsibility over the Area Health Authorities. These regional authorities were strengthened and made executives in the consultative paper published by the Conservative Government in

1971 after it came back into power.[20] In this respect, the Conservatives strengthened the trend towards centralization that already existed in the previous papers.

It is worth noting that the first Green Paper's initial intention of abolishing the regional tier was based on the desire to de-emphasize the influence of the hospital sector over the NHS as a whole.[21] Indeed, Labour spokesmen had often argued that the Regional Hospital Board (the pre-RHC body) was dominated by hospital and consultant interests. And it was feared that the new regional authorities would be easy prey for these pressure groups. Thus, it was felt that it would be wiser to make the administrative units smaller than regional units so that the hospitals' influence could be counter-balanced by local and general practice interests. And, while in the second Green Paper it was suggested that the regional tier might be advisable after all, in planning for the entirety of health services, it was still felt that these authorities should have only advisory responsibilities.[22] The granting of executive powers to these regional bodies by the Conservatives was an attempt to strengthen the central management of the system. Thus, fourteen Regional Health Authorities were suggested, based on the belief that 'the central department's span of control over ninety area health authorities in England would be too wide to make managerial sense'.[23] *The strengthening of the regional tier on those conditions had as its effect the further strengthening of hospital dominance within the system*

The 1972 White Paper

The aim and objective of the reform, i.e., centralization of policy and strengthening of management, appeared quite clearly in the White Paper prepared by the Conservative Government.[24] It specified that there would be a single chain of command, closely following the pattern of the previous hospital service. In place of the Regional Hospital Boards, the document spoke of fourteen Regional Health Authorities (whose responsibilities roughly corresponded to the pre-1974 RHBs). They would be responsible for planning services within the regions (subject, of course, to national planning by the Secretary of DHSS) and for allocating resources among the next level of authorities, the Area Health Authorities. The RHAs would have direct control over capital investments as well as over the appointments of senior medical staff. A unique feature of the RHAs was that, unlike the RHBs, they included the teaching hospitals under their jurisdiction. Actually, each region was supposed to be centred around one or more teaching hospitals.

The ninety Area Health Authorities were to assume the responsibilities held by the pre-1974 Hospital Management Committees and take over some of the pre-1974 local authorities' services (such as community nursing), as well as the planning of general practitioners' services. Under the new AHAs, however, the general practitioners were to retain their independent contractor status. Theirs was to be much the same situation as existed pre-1974. The AHA would not have any authority over the general practitioners, nor would it be able to reallocate resources between family practitioners and other services. As Brown has rightly indicated, this would leave the general practitioners exactly where they were before.[25]

The direct administrative responsibilities of the AHAs would be carried out by their District Management Teams, of which there are 206, normally based on district general hospitals. It is worth stressing that the district boundaries did not coincide with the political boundaries of the local governmental districts, nor with the local authorities' social services. This structure was clearly defined and the lines of authority were made quite explicit, i.e., direction from the top down and accountability from the bottom up. As the White Paper clearly specifies:

> In future, there will be a clear line of responsibility for the whole NHS from the Secretary of State to the RHAs and through them to the AHAs, with corresponding accountability from area to region to centre. The overall responsibility which will rest on the Secretary of State makes it necessary that, in addition to making statutory regulations and issuing guidance, he should be able to give formal direction to RHAs and AHAs.[26]

The aim of that reorganization was not, then, to integrate care — as most medical care researchers assume — but primarily to centralize management, to such a degree that fears arose that the plan was nurturing a 'bureaucratic monster', and paving the way for what an editorial in the *Sunday Times* ominously termed 'the onset of 1984'.[27] It also had a touch of American-developed 'no-nonsense managerialism', acquired through the role of the ubiquitous U.S. consultant firm of McKinsey Company, which contributed substantially to the elaboration of the Bill.[28]

By the end of the reorganization, the tripartite structure and administration of the NHS still existed, with (1) the hospital sector in a dominant position, prepared to spend the greatest part of the NHS budget; (2) the general practice services forced back into isolation; and (3) the local health departments of the local authorities further weakened and with fewer responsibilities. It is interesting to note that following each reform the shift in responsibility and power has been towards ad hoc bodies — controlled by class and professional interests, accountable to the central government — and away from the local authorities' control. And, contrary to what the report of the Royal Commission on Local Government (or Redcliffe-Maud Report) had advocated, i.e., the administration of the health services by the local government, the reorganization of these services meant a weakening of that administration, and a further division of authority for providing services. Most of the personal preventive services were delegated to the AHAs and the remaining ones were transferred to the new social service department, as the Seebohm Report had recommended. The local authorities were left with the responsibilities for primarily environmental health services.

Final Comments and Conclusions on the 1974 Reorganization

I am aware, of course, that my interpretation of both the origins and the nature of the 1974 reform differs from the one usually presented in medical care circles. Indeed, it is frequently assumed in such circles that this reform came into being as a result of pressures from within the NHS for integrating the three branches of that service. Disagreeing with this interpretation, I have indicated that the origin of the 1974 reform must be seen as emanating from *outside* the NHS, and very much rooted in the economic crises of the 1960's, as well as in the Labour leadership's political commitment to saving the capitalist economy. That commitment implied a centralization of social policies and the further strengthening of the centre's hold over the periphery through the creation of ad hoc regional and local bodies directly accountable to the central authority. In that respect, and as I have indicated previously, this trend towards centralization also occurred in other countries, such as the U.S., where the National Health Planning and Resource Development Act was passed, and ad hoc regional bodies directly accountable to the

Secretary of the Department of Health, Education and Welfare were created.

That the integration of care was not a primary aim of the 1974 reform is further demonstrated by the fact that the White Paper did not even propose integration of the three branches of the NHS. Instead, it perpetuated this three-part structure, with the services of the general practitioners, hospitals and local authorities remaining separate and autonomous. The general practitioners were to be administered by the renamed Family Practices Committees (corresponding closely to the previous Executive Councils), and the hospital services by the Regional and Area Health Authorities. And the scope of local authorities' services was seriously curtailed as a result of the delegation of many of their previous responsibilities to the hospitals. *Within these three branches, the most powerful one continued to be the hospital sector, whose dominance was further reinforced through the strengthening of centralization and management.*

What have been the consequences of the 1974 reorganization? In my opinion, *the strengthening of the central power of management of the NHS has determined a further deepening of, primarily, the class dominance and, secondarily, the professional dominance of this system.* Indeed, members of the ad hoc bodies of the RHAs and AHAs are selected for their 'managerial skills'. Not unlike previous bodies of this type (the RHBs and the HMCs),[29] their members are supposed to come primarily from the upper class, since such representatives are presumably the ones who know best how to manage and allocate resources and can speak on equal terms with the professionals. As Sir Keith Joseph, the Conservative Secretary of State for Health and Social Services indicated, the NHS needed small boards made up of those with 'managerial ability' — usually code words for people of the presumably respectable, mature and responsible upper class.[30] And the nature of the appointments showed this clearly. As J. Tudor Hart recently wrote of these appointments:

> Of 281 appointees named [by the Secretary of State for Social Services to the new English area and regional health authorities], 78 are bankers, company directors, business executives, property developers, and brokers; 39 are doctors; and there are 19 solicitors, six accountants, five retired Army officers, three ex-colonial governors, and 24 other professionals. Representing the sons of toil we have six farmers (one lord and one knight), 11 shopkeepers, 10 supervisory staff, 18 full-time trade union officials, three

> railwaymen, one coalminer, and one engineer. There are four of unstated occupation, and as most of the 53 women are listed as housewives they are difficult to classify; it seems unlikely that many of them have spent months waiting for an outpatient appointment, or spent hours waiting to see an overworked registrar, while a friend tries to cope with three children on top of her own.[31]

And, as another observer has indicated,

> Yet of a total of over 40 million persons receiving health care in Great Britain, those decision makers [those that sit in the planning and regulating authorities as well as in the executive management committees of the health institutions] can hardly be said to be representative. While one hesitates to question their judgment, they might reasonably be asked to declare their interests. That a title such as Dowager Viscountess should confer not only social graces, but a working knowledge of health care organization and the needs of most patients, is an assumption too often made by the titled few for the ungraced many.[32]

A consistent upper class and professional dominance appears again in the newly created RHAs and AHAs. Almost half of the new chairmen of the RHAs, appointed by Sir Keith Joseph, were presidents, managers, and directors of a varied assortment of companies. As Robson has indicated, the trend towards increasing corporate involvement is being reflected in that company directors have replaced doctors as the single largest occupational group. And a similar composition appears in the AHAs with over 30% of chairmen being company directors, as well as the usual ranks of lords, ladies, and ex-colonial governors.[33] The predominance of corporate directors and representatives of other fractions of the upper class does not mean, of course, that the medical profession has been left aside. They, and primarily the part-time private consultants, are well represented in those RHAs and AHAs.[34] And at the level of implementation — the District Management Teams — representatives of the consultants and general practitioners have the power to veto team decisions.[35] Moreover, a series of medical advisory bodies were established at the district, area, and regional levels, and the authorities were instructed to consult them.

Consumer and Citizen Participation in the Reorganized NHS

At this point, we might well ask where the general population fits into this reorganization, i.e., patients and potential patients. As to the former, the initial document gives the impression of being totally unaware of their existence. Consistent with its managerial tone and style, patients are nowhere to be found in that reorganization. As a consultative document bluntly reflected: 'For our purposes, patients are not part of the organization'.[36]

And regarding the latter — potential patients or the population — their appearance in the structure takes the form of a mere afterthought, and their input into the system is very limited indeed. Actually, it is interesting to note that this absence of local popular participation has been presented as a progressive measure, since local people are considered to be too conservative. Battistella and Chester, for example, indicate that from a purely sociological point of view,

> local communities are inherently conservative because of the high degree of internal cohesiveness and homogeneity which causes them to resist change and be less tolerant of deviations from normative standards of acceptable thought and behaviour.[37]

Instead the popular participation is supposed to take place through the four elected representatives of the local authorities (out of a total of fourteen members) that sit on the AHAs, as well as through the Community Health Councils (CHCs) which are merely advisory bodies to the District Management Teams and meet at least once a year.

Initially, the proposal establishing those Councils suggested that half of the CHCs' members should be appointed by the local authorities and half by the AHAs, the mother agencies of the bodies (the District teams) that were supposed to be supervised by the Councils. Moreover, the funds for the operation of those Councils were presumably to come from the AHAs. Under pressure, the composition was changed so that half were nominated by local authorities, one third were chosen by voluntary organizations, and one sixth were selected by the Regional Health Authorities, with responsibility for financing the CHCs to be transferred from the AHAs to the Regional Health Authority, the Regional body responsible for planning the activities of those teams.[38] Having not executive responsibilities but merely advisory ones, and with their funding provided by the planning agencies, the bodies that they were supposed to supervise, they have been perceived as 'relatively powerless'.[39] There is indeed a very limited, almost meaningless, popular input into the new NHS. These Councils can be perceived as the fig leaves on the naked managerial body of the NHS. As Barbara Castle has indicated, they are the bodies 'stuck on at the bottom to give the semblance of democracy'.[40]

Not surprisingly, some sectors of the labour movement have criticized the present structure on the basis of its absence of popular participation and input into the decision-making and management of health services.[41]

The proposed changes by the Labour Government, presented in the document somewhat hyperbolically entitled 'Democracy in the NHS', published in May of 1974, did not substantially change that lack of popular control of the NHS.[42] The changes suggested by the Labour Government indicated that

1) the CHCs should elect two voting members to each of the AHAs;
2) one-third of the AHAs and RHAs were to be members of the local authorities;
3) two members of the hospital staff other than physicians were to serve on each of the AHAs and RHAs; and
4) a national council of CHCs was to be established.

But, as Blair has indicated, these changes, while representing an advancement, still have not corrected the overwhelming class and professional dominance of these AHAs and RHAs.[43] Moreover, that class dominance appears in the CHCs as well. Less than 30% of those Councils, originally supposed to represent the interest of the communities, were composed of members of the working class, which included in 1971 over 70% of the U.K. population.[44] The social class bias of those Councils would explain, at least partially, the non-conflictive nature of the Councils. As Ham indicates:

> . . . the majority of CHCs have tended towards the consensual end of the role spectrum. They exhibit many of the attitudes formerly associated with HMCs, are deferential to officers, . . . and espouse a philosophy which emphasizes responsibility.[45]

That non-conflictive nature was also observed by an author of a review on the experiences of the CHCs in northern England. He indicated that, 'On the whole, the Councils have been too polite and deferential'.[46]

It is worth stressing that other nationalized industries have had advisory consultative councils for years, and that they have been proved highly ineffective in representing the consumers' interests.

Similar to the CHCs, those councils have been found not to have much power, and, as a whole, not to be representative of the community. They have tended to be 'subservient to the nationalized industry concerned, communicating producers' viewpoints to consumers instead of the reverse, and reacting to laws from above rather than formulating their own, alternative, policies'.[47]

Given the current structure, the only mechanism of popular participation is nationwide, through national general elections and the opportunity to change the governing party. But, as Bevan himself indicated, 'If you close the avenues between the citizens and the state (and its branches, such as the NHS) in between elections, then you must realize that human beings are not going to have the patience to sit down in resignation for five years until they have another chance'.[48] But, it was Bevan himself who failed to provide for the mechanism of community and worker participation, much less control of the NHS. That absence of popular control of the NHS appears clearly, not only in the present structure, but in the genesis and development of the reorganization of the NHS. Indeed, the latter in large degree explains the former. The 1971 Conservative consultative document — the one that determined the final form of the restructuring — was not even published by the HMSO (the government printing office). Instead it was made available only to interested parties. The meaning of this is made quite clear by Willcocks' comment that 'this technique in itself is a curious compliment to the pressure groups and an equally curious rejection of the general public's possible interests in any reform'.[49]

NOTES

1 Department of Health and Social Security, *National Health Service Reorganization,* London, Her Majesty's Stationery Office, Command Paper 5055 (1972).

2 R. Battistella and T.E. Chester, 'The 1974 Reorganization of the British National Health Service — Aims and Issues', *The New England Journal of Medicine* (September 10, 1973), p. 610; and S. Jonas and D. Banta, 'The 1974 Reorganization of the British National Health Service: An Analysis', *Journal of Community Health*, 1(2) (Winter 1975), p. 91.

3 Among the reports that are frequently mentioned as precursors of the reorganization is the Porritt Report, prepared by a committee on which academic medicine was predominant. Sir Arthur Porritt, *A Review of the Medical Services in Great Britain: Report of a Medical Review Committee Established by the British Medical Association and the Various Consultant Colleges under the Chairmanship of Sir Arthur Porritt*, London (1962).

4 Miliband, *op. cit.,* p. 339.

5 Quoted in *Ibid.*, p. 339.

6 *Labour Party Annual Conference Report* (1959), p. 109.

7 A. Crosland, *The Future of Socialism*, London, Jonathan Cape Ltd. (1956).

8 *Labour Party Annual Conference Report* (1959), p. 122.

9 D.E. Butler and R. Rose, *The British General Election of 1959*, London, Macmillan (1960), p. 17.

10 *Ibid.*, p. 70.

11 Butler and A. King, *The British General Election of 1964*. London, Macmillan (1965), p. 135.

12 Butler and King, *The British General Election of 1966*, London, Macmillan (1967).

13 For the political origins of the economic crises of Britain and their relationship to the state of class struggle, see A. Glyn and B. Sutcliffe, *British Capitalism, Workers, and the Profit Squeeze*, London, Penguin (1972).

14 Child Poverty Action Group, *Poverty and the Labour Government*, London (1970). Also, see P. Townsend and N. Bosanquet (eds.), *Labour and Inequality*, London, The Fabian Society (1972).

15 R.G.S. Brown, *The Changing National Health Service*, London, Routledge and Kegan Paul (1973), p. 81.

16 Royal Commission on Local Government in England, *Report, Volume I*, London, Her Majesty's Stationery Office, Command Paper 4040 (1968).

17 Ministry of Health, *National Health Service: The Administrative Structure of the Medical and Related Services in England and Wales*, London, Her Majesty's Stationery Office (1968).

18 Department of Health and Social Security, *National Health Service: The Future Structure of the NHS*, London, Her Majesty's Stationery Office (1970).

19 Brown, *op. cit.*, p. 71. Also R. Kohn, 'The Reorganization of the British National Health Service: A Largely Frustrated Case Study', *International Journal of Health Services* (in process).

20 Department of Health and Social Security, *National Health Service Reorganization: Consultative Document*, London, Her Majesty's Stationery Office (1971).

21 B. Abel-Smith. Communication to the author.

22 Brown, *op. cit.*, p. 75.

23 Quoted in Kohn, *op. cit.*

24 Department of Health and Social Security, *National Health Service Reorganization, op. cit.*

25 Brown, *op. cit.*, p. 74.

26 Quoted in P. Draper and T. Smart, 'Social Science and Health Policy in the United Kingdom: Some Contributions of the Social Sciences to the Bureaucratization of the National Health Service', *International Journal of Health Services*, 4 (Summer 1974), p. 454.

27 Quoted in *Ibid.*, p. 455.

28 *Ibid.*, p. 454.

29 Of the 15 Chairmen of the RHB in 1964, 11 were either directors, partners, or chairmen in one or more of 50 different companies. In the Boards studied, the single largest occupational group besides that of doctors, was that of company directors. Of the total number of members of the Board, only one was an industrial worker. Similarly for the HMCs, of the 360 Chairmen, one-quarter were company directors, with the composition of the Boards including 4 lord lieutenants, 20 deputy lieutenants, 146 JPs, 12 peers or baronets, 5 wives, widows, or offspring of peers, 1 retired ambassador, 1 ex-lord mayor, and many generals and admirals. M. Stewart, *Unpaid Public Science*. London, Fabian Pamphlet, No 3 (1964).

30 Brown, *op. cit.*, p. 75.

31 J. Tudor Hart, 'Industry and the Health Service', *The Lancet*, ii(7829) (1973).

32 J. Robson, 'The NHS Company, Inc.? The Social Consequence of the Professional Dominance in the National Health Service', *op. cit.*

33 *Ibid.*

34 *Ibid.*

35 Brown, *op. cit.*

36 Quoted in Draper and Smart, *op. cit.*, p. 456.

37 R. Battistella and T. Chester, 'Reorganization of the National Health Service: Background and Issues in England's Quest for a Comprehensive—Integrated Planning and Delivery System', *Health and Society* (Fall 1973), pp. 526-527.

38 R. Klein and J. Lewis, 'The Politics of Consumer Representatives. A Study of Community Health Councils', London, Centre for Studies in Social Policy (1976), p. 16.

39 Levitt, *op. cit.*, p. 191. Also see M. Stacey, 'The Health Service Consumer: A Sociological Misconception', in M. Stacey (ed.), *The Sociology of the NHS*, Sociological Review Monograph, University of Keele (1976).

40 Castle, *op. cit.*, p. 10.

41 D. McKie, 'Labour and the NHS', *The Lancet*, ii(7833) (1973), p. 841.

42 Department of Health and Social Security, *Democracy in the National Health Service,* London, Her Majesty's Stationery Office (1974).

43 I. Blair, 'Private Practice. Notes on a Growth Industry', *Medicine in Society*, 1(3) (1974), p. 42.

44 Klein and Lewis, *op. cit.,* p. 61.

45 C.J. Ham, 'Power, Patients, and Pluralism', in K. Barnard and K. Lee (eds.), *Conflicts in the National Health Service*, London, Croom Helm (1977), p. 103.

46 J. Hallan, *CHCs in Action*, London, Nuffield Provincial Hospitals Trust (1976), p. 59.

47 Ham, *op cit.,* p. 104.

48 Quoted in Kohn, *op. cit.*

49 Willcocks, 'Decision Making and Interest Groups in the National Health Service', in Learmonth, *op. cit.,* p. 141.

PART II

Growth, Equity and Effectiveness in the Medical Care Sector in Today's Great Britain

CHAPTER VII

The Composition and Distribution of Medical Resources in Great Britain

Introduction

In both the daily press and the academic literature of Western capitalist societies, there is currently much discussion and debate on three issues related to the medical care sector of those societies.

The first controversy is a result of the very rapid growth in the consumption of societal resources on the part of the medical care sector. Through its use of scarce capital — capital that, it is argued, could be more productively and profitably invested in the private and productive sectors of the economy — the medical sector's expenditures are assumed to be greatly contributing to the crises currently plaguing the Western capitalist economies.

The second issue, and one widely discussed in both lay and professional circles, involves what is perceived to be the maldistribution of medical care resources. Indeed, a concern is presently being voiced that, in addition to spending too much on the medical care sector, we may also be spending that money unwisely and inequitably. It is generally assumed that while social class inequities of consumption have been practically overcome due to welfare state measures, still others (inequities of consumption by age group, region, and type of care, for example) are considered to persist and to represent cause for alarm.

And last but not least, the third concern has to do with the issue of effectiveness. Because of the widespread assumption — and a wrong one at that — that medical care has as its primary objective the reduction of mortality and morbidity, increasing frustration is being expressed as a result of the observation that there does not seem to be any direct relationship between the amount of medical care that is consumed and the population's general level of health. And this concern is frequently accompanied by a parallel concern that medical care, at this point and in this period, may perhaps be doing more harm than good.

In the analysis of these three related issues — growth of medical care expenditures, inequities in the consumption of these expenditures, and the relative effectiveness of such investments — much attention has been focused on forces, such as professional dominance of the health sector, that emerge *within* the medical sector and that are considered to be responsible for its problems. Elsewhere, I have presented a critique of such interpretations.[1] Suffice it to repeat here that, disagreeing with these theories, I believe that in order to explain the enormous growth of the social expenditures, including health expenditures, in our Western capitalist societies, as well as the inequitable and ineffective pattern of consumption of these expenditures, we have to go *outside* the health sector and study the main economic and political forces that determine the nature of our capitalist societies and of our medical care sectors. And the main scenario for the understanding of the interplay of these forces is the analysis of class relations.

The Class Structure and Class Relations of Britain Today

Let us start, then, by describing very briefly the class structure and class relations in Great Britain. At the very top of that society, we find a small percentage of the population which owns a disproportionate share of the personal wealth. According to the Cambridge economist, J.S. Revell, and reported in *The Economist*, in 1960 the top 1% of British adults (roughly 250,000 people) owned 42% of Britain's total personal wealth, the top 5% owned 75%, the top 10% owned 83%,[2] and the top 12% owned 96% of all wealth.[3] Subsequent studies show that there has not been any meaningful change in this very skewed pattern of wealth distribution. In this respect, *The Economist* opened one of its editorials, significantly entitled 'The Indefensible Status Quo', with the sentence: 'There is undoubtedly a permanent built-in tendency to inequality here . . .' and went on to assert that the system of British taxation (elaborated, designed, and implemented by both Labour and Conservative governments) represents 'a system which over the past sixty years . . . has not only failed in its original aim of breaking up the big fortunes, but has also done far too little to help the building up of small ones'.[4]

The upper class has historically been, and continues to be, a steady force in British society, and one very much at the centre of things. Its two main components are the land owning aristocracy and gentry on the one hand, and financial and industrial capital on the other — groups that are increasingly interrelated.[5] They are the owners of land and the holders of stock in large financial and manufacturing corporations.[6]

At the other end of the social spectrum is the working class, comprised primarily of industrial or blue collar workers, workers in the services sector, and also agricultural wage earners. Table 7.1, demonstrating the changes from 1911 to 1981 (estimated) of the occupational groupings of the British working population, shows that, contrary to widely held belief, manual workers (skilled, semi-skilled, and unskilled) do represent the majority of the British labour force —67.5% of that force, to be precise.

In terms of absolute figures, the number of industrial wage earners fell from 9,800,000 in 1951 to 9,600,000 in 1961 — not much of a fall, however, for at this rate there would be a drop in twenty-five years of only about a half-million. And if agricultural workers are added in the totals become 10,550,000 for 1951 and 10,100,000 for 1961. This slow decline of industrial and agricultural workers has been more than compensated for by the growth of non-industrial manual workers (e.g., local government manual workers such as refuse collectors), from 2¾ million in 1951 to over 3 million in 1961. In summary, the working class (manual wage earners) represents the majority of the British labour force and of the British population, and is likely to continue to do so for quite a while.[7]

In between the 'polar classes', there is the middle class, consisting of (1) the professionals, including doctors, lawyers, academicians, etc., whose main common denominator is that their work is intellectual as opposed to manual, and usually requires professional training; (2) the business middle class, who are the owners and controllers of the competitive sector of the British economy, are associated with small and medium-sized enterprises, and range from businessmen employing a few workers to owners of fairly sizeable enterprises of every kind; (3) the self-employed shopkeepers, craftsmen, and artisans — a declining sector of the labour force; and (4) the clerical workers, the group that has grown most rapidly within the labour force in the last two decades, and which accounts for the majority of white collar workers.[8]

For reasons of brevity, and accepting the simplifications that this categorization implies, I will continue, in this book, to refer to

TABLE 7.1 *Distribution by Occupations and Occupational Earnings of the Labour Force in Great Britain, 1911–1981*

Occupations listed as % of total distribution
Occupations (Women Only) listed as % of total occupied women(1)
Earnings (Men Only) listed as % of overall average
Earnings (Women Only) listed as average for all women in the same period(2)

	Occupations 1911	*Occupations 1921 (Women Only)*	*Occupations 1931*	*Occupations 1951*	*Earnings 1955/56 (Men Only)*
Employers	4.1	N.A.	3.5	2.0	N.A.
Self-employed (non manual)	2.7	N.A.	3.4	3.0	N.A.
Professional:	4.0	15.4	4.6	6.6	N.A.
(Higher)	N.A.	(2.0)(3)	N.A.	N.A.	243
(Lower)	N.A.	(13.4)	N.A.	N.A.	96
Managers	3.3		3.5	5.5	284
(Sub-total of above)	(14.1)	–	(15.0)	(17.1)	N.A.
Clerks	4.8	16.3(4)	7.0	10.7	82
Foremen/Supervisors	1.3	} 24.4 (Foremen/Supervisors and Skilled Manual)	1.5	2.6	124
Skilled Manual	30.6		26.7	24.9	98
Semi-Skilled	39.5	38.5(5)	35.0	32.6	74
Unskilled	9.6	5.4	14.8	12.8	69
Totals	100%	100%	100%	100%	–

(1) The percentage of women in the labour force, relative to that of men, was 43, 42, 43, 44 and 56%, in the periods 1913/14, 1922/24, 1935/36, 1955/56 and 1970 respectively.
(2) In 1955/56, women's earnings were 49% of those received by men, and by 1970, this had increased to 54%.
(3) Includes managers.
(4) Includes sales workers.

Sources: G. Routh, *Occupations and Pay in Great Britain* (1906–60); General Register Office, *Sample Census* (1966); Department of Employment, *Employment and Productivity Gazette*, March (1969); J. Westergaard and H. Resler, *Class in a Capitalist Society*, New York, Basic Books (1975).

groups (1) and (2) as the upper-middle class, and groups (3) and (4) as the lower-middle class.

Let me add, at this point, one note of clarification. That is, that many clerical workers are, either by association or pattern of consumption, members of the working class. Indeed, as Levinson[9] has shown for the equivalent category of workers in the U.S., the majority of women clerical workers are married to working class men, and thus share the culture and values of that class.[10]

Earnings 1960 (Women Only)	*Occupations 1961 (Women Only)*	*Occupations 1966*	*Occupations 1966 (Women Only)*	*Earnings 1970 (Men Only)*	*Occupations 1971 (Women Only)*	*Occupations 1981 (Est.)*
N.A.	N.A.	4.2	4.1[3]	N.A.	4.7[3]	–
N.A.	N.A.		N.A.	N.A.	N.A.	–
–	16.2	7.0	48.5	N.A.	49.6	–
(327)	(0.9)[3]	N.A.	(0.8)[8]	252	(0.6)[8]	–
139	(15.3)	N.A.	(47.7)[9]	105	(49.0)[9]	–
228[6]		6.2		230		–
–	–	(17.4)	–	–	–	(20.0)
97	37.3[4]	11.5	N.A.	85	N.A.	16.0
138[7]	9.4	2.8	10.5[10]	126	9.0[10]	
91		57.5		99		23.0
78	35.4[5]		29.3[5]	72	28.0[5]	30.0
64	1.7	10.0	7.6	67	8.7	11.0
–	100%	100%	100%	–	100%	100%

(5) Includes personal service workers, who represented 28.7% of total occupied women in 1921, 18.8% in 1961, 13.6% in 1966 and 14.3% in 1971.
(6) Includes administrators.
(7) Forewomen only.
(8) Classified as 'major professions'.
(9) Includes both intermediate and junior non-manual workers.
(10) Includes own account workers.

The Class Structure in the Medical Care Sector

This class structure, with its subsequent hierarchicalization, also appears in the medical sector. Indeed, as we have seen in the first part of this volume, members of the upper and upper-middle classes predominate in the decision-making bodies (RHAs and AHAs) of the NHS. As for the producers and members of the labour force in the health sector, Table 7.2 shows their distribution. At the very top, we find

TABLE 7.2 *Persons Employed in the Delivery of Health Services in England, by Sex and by Salary, in 1972*

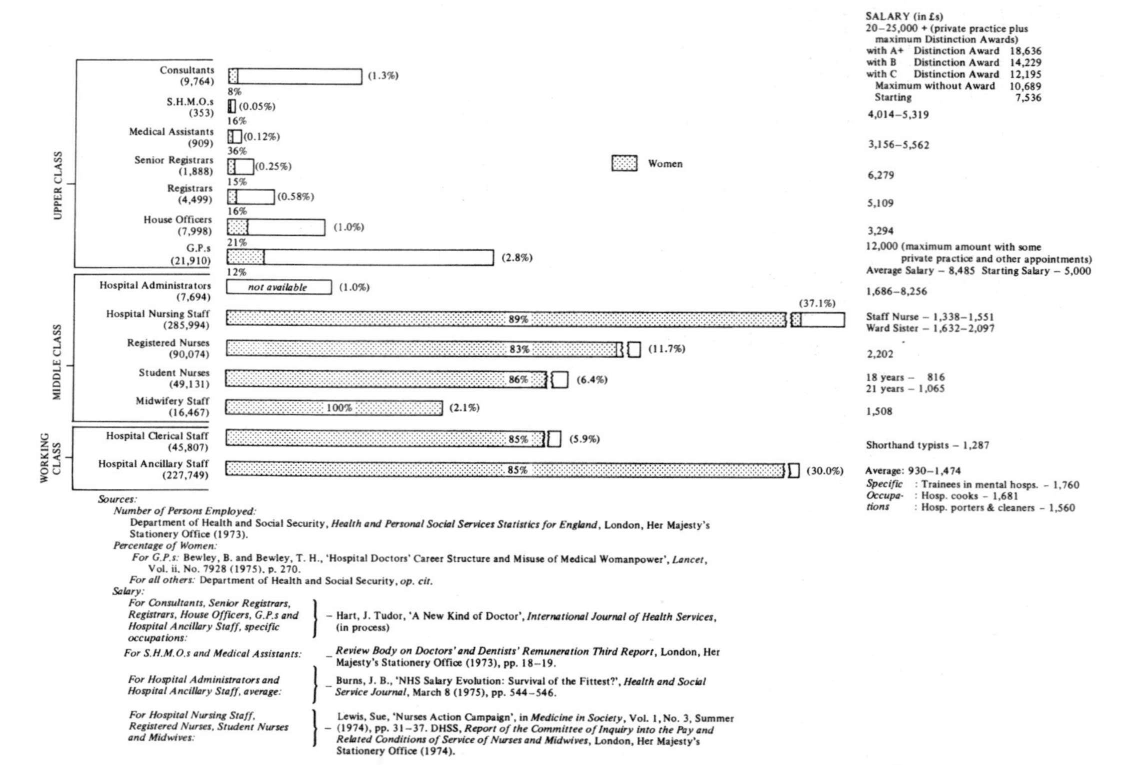

Sources:

Number of Persons Employed:
Department of Health and Social Security, *Health and Personal Social Services Statistics for England*, London, Her Majesty's Stationery Office (1973).

Percentage of Women:
For G.P.s: Bewley, B. and Bewley, T. H., 'Hospital Doctors' Career Structure and Misuse of Medical Womanpower', *Lancet*, Vol. ii, No. 7928 (1975), p. 270.
For all others: Department of Health and Social Security, *op. cit.*

Salary:
For Consultants, Senior Registrars, Registrars, House Officers, G.P.s and Hospital Ancillary Staff, specific occupations: – Hart, J. Tudor, 'A New Kind of Doctor', *International Journal of Health Services*, (in process)

For S.H.M.O.s and Medical Assistants: – *Review Body on Doctors' and Dentists' Remuneration Third Report*, London, Her Majesty's Stationery Office (1973), pp. 18–19.

For Hospital Administrators and Hospital Ancillary Staff, average: – Burns, J. B., 'NHS Salary Evolution: Survival of the Fittest?', *Health and Social Service Journal*, March 8 (1975), pp. 544–546.

For Hospital Nursing Staff, Registered Nurses, Student Nurses and Midwives: – Lewis, Sue, 'Nurses Action Campaign', in *Medicine in Society*, Vol. 1, No. 3, Summer (1974), pp. 31–37. DHSS, *Report of the Committee of Inquiry into the Pay and Related Conditions of Service of Nurses and Midwives*, London, Her Majesty's Stationery Office (1974).

the hospital-based physicians or consultants, whose income from the NHS includes their basic salary, as well as the different types of merit awards described earlier. Behind the consultant is the one who, in Lord Moran's terminology, has not completely made it within the system — the general practitioner, whose different levels of income are presented in Table 7.2. These two groups represent the upper and upper-middle classes in the medical profession. Table 7.3 shows how the median weekly earnings of those in the medical profession compare with the earnings of other members of the upper and upper-middle classes who are in different occupations.[11]

Below, much below, we find the lower-middle class (i.e., nurses, therapists, technologists, and technicians), a group that represents 39% of the labour force in the health sector, and is primarily female. And below this group, we find the working class per se of the health sector — auxiliary, ancillary, and service personnel — who comprise 54.2% of the health labour force, are predominantly female (84.1%) and include an over-representation of foreign workers (the 'blacks' of Britain).

TABLE 7.3 *Gross Weekly Earnings of Adult Full-time Male Employees in Selected Occupations, 1971*

Occupational Groups (male full-time employees only, pay not affected by absence)	*Median Gross Weekly Earnings (£)*
Managers – general and divisional	69.6
Company chairmen and directors	66.5
Medical and Dental Practitioners	**58.4**
University Academic Staff	57.7
Managers – marketing, advertising, sales	52.7
Managers – personnel and training	47.1
Architects and planners	47.2
Solicitors	46.2
Teachers in further education	44.8
Accountants	43.4
Managers – works and production	42.8
Engineers, scientists, technologists	41.4
Managers – office	40.9

Source: Department of Employment *Gazette*, December (1971), pp. 1150–52, 1157–59: data from New Survey of Earnings, April (1971).

It is worth mentioning at this point that, as in all other Western capitalist societies, the system of education in Britain, including the education of those in the medical and paramedical professions, perpetuates social roles already in existence within the predefined class structure. Indeed, Simpson[12] and Robson[13] have shown that (a) the social class backgrounds of the main groups within the health labour force have not changed during the last twenty-five years, and (b) education fixes and perpetuates these social backgrounds and replicates existing social roles. Simpson, for example, mentions that within the five-scale grouping of classes in Britain, the offspring of social classes 1 and 2 (equivalent to the upper and upper-middle classes, as defined above) predominate in medicine:

> In 1961 more than a third were from class 2, rather less than a third from class 3, and only 3% from classes 4 and 5 together. By 1966, social class 1 was contributing nearly 40%. The proportion of children of classes 1 and 2 in universities generally, derived from the Robbins Report, is about 59%. Individual medical schools vary between 69 and 73%. It is hard to believe that the small number of medical students selected from families of low average income exhausts the potentially good students contained in this large part of the population.[14]

That this situation may even follow a predefined policy is indicated in the following statement from the Royal College of Surgeons:

> . . . there has always been a nucleus in medical schools of students from cultured homes . . . This nucleus has been responsible for the continued high social prestige of the profession as a whole and for the maintenance of medicine as a learned profession. Medicine would lose immeasurably if the proportion of such students in the future were to be reduced in favour of the precocious children who qualify for subsidies from the Local Authorities and State purely on examination results.[15]

Let me clarify here that this absence of social mobility within the health labour force reflects the overall lack of mobility in British society, clearly shown by J. Westergaard and H. Resler.[16] Today, as in the past, and as Harold Laski used to say, the careful selection of one's own parents remains among the most important variables determining one's power, wealth, income, and opportunities in Great Britain. And this is as much true for the medical care sector as everywhere else.

Moreover, this class structure and the relations it determines establish the scenario within which it is possible to understand the evolution, growth, composition and distribution of resources in the medical care sector. Regarding the evolution of the medical sector, we saw in Part I of this volume that the nature and structure of health and social legislation — from the Lloyd George Act of 1911 to the 1974 NHS reorganization — were in large degree determined by the evolution and level of the confrontation, born of the capitalist mode of production, among all social classes, but primarily between the capitalist and the working classes. In Part II, I will show how the growth, composition and distribution of resources in the NHS are also primarily determined by the class structure and by the class relations of British society.

The Growth of the Public Sector

A most dramatic event in the evolution of capitalism over the past five decades — but particularly accentuated in the last decade — has been the steady growth of public expenditure, primarily in the areas of health, education and government. Table 7.4 shows the growth of employment, for example, in the various sectors of the British economy. We can see that while agriculture and mining have

TABLE 7.4 *Industrial Distribution of the Labour Force in Great Britain, 1911–1981 (In Percentages)*

Industrial Category	*1911*	*1931*	*1951*	*1966*	*1981 (est.)*
Agriculture	8.5	6.0	5.0	3.0	2.5
Mining	6.5	5.5	4.0	2.5	0.5
Manufacturing, of which	34.0	35.0	37.0	36.0	33.0
(Engineering and Electrical)	(5.0)	(5.5)	(8.0)	(9.0)	(8.0)
(Vehicles, etc.)	(1.5)	(2.0)	(4.5)	(4.0)	(4.0)
(Metals, etc.)	(4.5)	(5.0)	(5.5)	(5.0)	(4.0)
Building and Utilities	6.0	6.5	8.0	9.5	9.0
Transport and Distribution	20.0	21.5	20.0	20.5	23.0
Government and Services	**25.0**	**25.5**	**26.0**	**28.5**	**32.0**
TOTAL	100.0%	100.0%	100.0%	100.0%	100.0%

Source: G. Routh, *Occupations and Pay in Great Britain, 1906–60*; General Register Office, *Sample Census, 1966*; and Department of Employment, *Employment and Productivity Gazette*, March (1969), for 1981 estimates.

TABLE 7.5 *State Employees in Great Britain 1955–1968*

(In Thousands)

	1955			*1968*			*Total % Change 1955–68 1955 = 100*
	Male	*Female*	*Total*	*Male*	*Female*	*Total*	
1. *Public Administration*							
H.M. Forces	790	19	809	380	15	395	
National Government	399	164	553	382	212	594	107
Local Government	540	186	726	608	225	833	114
Total Civil	939	350	1279	990	437	1427	112
Total	1729	369	2088	1370	452	1822	87
2. *Educational, Medical and Dental Services*							
Education	329(1)	220(1)	678	423	922	1345	**199**
Medical and Dental	60(2)	200(2)	655	243	758	1001	**153**
Total	–	–	1333	666	1680	2346	**176**
3. *Nationalized Industries*							
Gas, Electricity, Water	338	40	378	360	57	417	110
Coal	–	–	704	485	21	506	72
Iron and Steel	260(3)	30(3)	290(3)	250	20	270	92(3)
Railways	–	–	506	275	23	298	59
Postal, etc.	–	–	308	323	120	543	176
Other	–	–	200(4)	–	–	240(4)	100(4)
Total	–	–	2386	–	–	2074	85

4. *Total Working Population*							
All Economically Active	16084	7828	23912	16285	8948	25233	106
Self-employed and Employers	916	62	978	1320	361	1681	172(5)
Employees	14257	7676	21933	14580	8572	23152	105
Unemployed	121	71	192	429	77	506	264
H.M. Forces	790	19	809	380	15	395	49
Total Civil State Employees	–	–	4998	–	–	5807	116

Notes: (1) Employees in direct grant and maintained or assisted schools and in universities, excluding further education and private schools.
(2) Doctors and nurses in the NHS respectively.
(3) Estimated as half of all working in metal manufacture.
(4) Estimates for road, sea and air transport, ports, etc.
(5) The basis for these figures is different in the two years.

Source: Department of Employment, *Gazette* (1969).

declined in numbers of employed, and manufacturing has remained almost constant, the building / utilities, transport / distribution, and above all, government / services sectors grew very dramatically between 1911 and 1966. And within the category of public employment, *the most substantial growth has been* (as shown in Table 7.5) *in the areas of local government, education, and medical and dental services.*

This expansion in public employment has gone side by side with an equally dramatic growth in public expenditure, with the percentage of the Gross National Product going towards such expenditure rising rapidly from only 13.5% in 1913 to 52.1% by 1968, and the percentage spent specifically on social services increasing from 4.7% to 26.0% in the same time period (Table 7.6).[17]

This growth of public expenditure is in large degree related, of course, to the dramatic increase in public employment. Indeed, while one-third of all public expenditure goes for purchasing goods and services,[18] two-thirds of these expenditures represent wages of state employees, whether soldiers, doctors, nurses or teachers.[19]

And this growth has not been restricted to Britain alone. As indicated in a recent report on present and estimated expenditures for the period 1960-1980 in the countries which are members of the Organisation for Economic Co-operation and Development:

> the most striking feature [in these countries] is the extent to which *education, health and social security* were responsible for the rising share of government expenditures over this period.[20]

It is clear that, as in most other Western capitalist countries, a major characteristic of British capitalism is a very dramatic growth in public expenditure, including health expenditures.

The most prevalent explanation for this growth is that the population's demand for social services has increased very substantially, forcing an expansion of both the allocative and productive policies of the state.[21] I find this explanation seriously limiting and limited, however, since it assumes that this demand is the *cause* of that growth, without analysing why such an increase in demand came about in the first place.

Contrary to this explanation, I believe that the growth of social expenditure is very much the result of (1) the social demands of the working population, on the one hand, and (2) the growth and monopolization of the process of capital accumulation, on the other. In

TABLE 7.6 *Public Expenditure in the United Kingdom, 1913–1968 (in £ million)*

	1913	*1923*	*1933*	*1948*	*1953*	*1958*	*1968*
Shares of G.N.P.							
G.N.P. (Factor cost)	2527	4178	4042	10468	15000	20408	36686
Public Expenditure	342	1154	1220	4210	6671	8308	19122
as % of G.N.P.	13.5	27.5	30	40.2	44.5	40.6	52.1
Current	241	933	1023	3630	5147	6516	14245
Capital	101	221	197	580	1524	1792	4877
Capital % of Total	29.5	19.0	16.0	14.0	23.0	21.5	25.5
Type of Expenditure as % of G.N.P.							
Debt Service	0.95	8.3	5.5	4.8	4.6	5.1	5.2
Military	3.0	4.7	3.8	7.4	11.5	7.6	6.7
Civil Government	0.8	1.3	1.4	2.3	2.5	2.1	2.8
Economic Services (of which	4.0	5.2	6.8	6.9	7.1	7.6	11.4
Public Corporations' Capital Formation)	–	–	–	(2.2)	(3.2)	(3.3)	(4.4)
Social Services*	4.7	8.0	12.5	18.6	18.8	18.2	26.0
TOTAL	13.5	27.5	30.0	40.2	44.5	40.6	52.1

**Note:* Social expenditure includes all public housing expenditure, current and capital, *gross* of rent receipts in this table.

Source: National Income and Expenditure *Blue Books* (1968); and London and Cambridge Economic Service, *Key Statistics, 1900–64.*

other words, the increase in public (including social) expenditure can be attributed to an intrinsic conflict between the demands of Labour and the needs of Capital (usually referred to as the need for capital accumulation). Due to the importance of each, let me further elaborate on them.

The Growth of the Social Demands of Labour

Labour movements in Britain have historically viewed social services (including health services) as part of the *social wage*, to be defended and increased in the same way that *money wages* are. Indeed, as we have seen in the previous section on the history of health legislation in Britain, the timing, structure, and nature of health legislation depend very much on the degree of militancy of the Labour Movement at the time. In the Labour-Capital conflict, the Labour Movement has demanded:

1. *An increase in social wages*, the comprehensiveness and level of which has depended on the strength of working class pressure. Consequently, the Labour Movement has fought for an expansion of social services, vigorously opposing any cuts in those social expenditures. The most recent example of this is the strike of coalminers in Yorkshire in order to protest at cuts in the NHS and support a rise in pay for nurses.[22] It is worth stressing that, following the pattern explained previously, the expansion of social expenditures in the NHS is, in large degree, due to both the growth of employment in social services and the growth of wages of service workers. Over 70% of the Health and Personal Social Services' (HPSS) current expenditures are for staff salaries and wages, which rose by 43% for hospital and community health service workers between November 1973 and November 1974. According to David Owen, then Secretary of the Department, this increase in wages and salaries was the major factor contributing to the rise of the GNP devoted to the NHS from 4.9% over the previous two years to 5.4% in 1975.[23] And that pattern of wage increase was a result of the heightening of labour militancy, including that among service workers. Indeed, the early 1970's saw an intensification of workers' militancy, as a result of declining real income in the late 1960's. A sign of that militancy was that, while the

annual average number of days lost due to strikes during the period 1960-1967 was 3,000,000 days, the comparable figure for the period from 1969 to 1972 was 12,000,000 days.[24] And most of the strikes were defensive, responding to a very real decline in real wages due to accelerating price increases and the growing burden of taxation.[25] Among the most affected workers were the service workers, including health service workers who had been chronically underpaid and who had presented a 'new militancy' in the early 1970's.[26]

2. *An increase in jobs*, so as to counteract the tendency towards unemployment characteristic of contemporary capitalism. The growth of employment, clearly shown in Table 7.5, reflects in large degree the demand upon the state to absorb the increasing surplus population. Also, the strong resistance presented by the Labour Movement to further cuts in social expenditure and in the public sector is determined by the fear of further increases in the rate of unemployment in the U.K., currently the highest rate since the Great Depression (5.2 percent in 1976).[27]

3. *Provision of services* — such as health services, social security, unemployment insurance, and the like — to smooth out and cushion the dislocation, uncertainty and diswelfare created by the process of capital accumulation, both in the process of production and consumption. Indeed, the paradox of the present welfare state is that it requires an expansion of itself in an attempt to solve the problems that it creates, problems, incidentally, that cannot be solved within the persisting pattern of class controls over those processes of production and consumption. Let's try to analyse, for example, three major health problems in today's Britain, and which are shared by all capitalist societies.

a. Alienation of the workers — the majority of citizens in British society — is responsible for the sizeable number of psychosomatic conditions seen in medical practices, and is largely due to the lack of control felt by the workers over their own work and over societal institutions. Work, for example, a most important activity in the lives of the majority of our population, serves primarily not as an opportunity for creativity or self-expression, but rather as a means of obtaining one's satisfaction elsewhere — in the world of consumption, where that self-expression is supposed to take place. But such self-expression can never be realized, since the world of consumption is based on the stimulation of wants; as Marcuse, in his *One Dimensional Man*, has pointed out, we all have to aspire to more where more always has to be inaccessible. A continuous process of alienation and frustration is created by the capitalist system that reflects itself in despair and much disease and frustration. That disease and unease creates a demand by the workers on the health services that can, at least, ameliorate the damage created by his or her relationship with the process of capital accumulation and the set of collective and personal relationships that it determines.

b. Occupational diseases that have been defined as 'the new plague' in modern society. In the U.K. every year, 2,000 workers are killed at work or are dying of disease contracted at work; 70,000 workers are seriously injured by cutting instruments; 796,000 workers are injured each year, which includes 19,533 fractures, 14,455 lacerations, 1,799 contusions, 1,489 amputations, 1,096 dislocations, etc., etc., etc.[28] The aetiology of these conditions is very much the result of control over the labour process by Capital and not by Labour, with capital accumulation taking priority over job safety and workers' satisfaction. Faced with that reality, the workers demand an increased protection that determines an expansion of the modes of state intervention. The limited intervention by the state, as well as the pro-Capital bias of that intervention, shows — as I will further explain in Part III — the hegemonic influence that Capital has over the organs of the state. That influence determines the extremely poor efficacy of most of the work safety regulations in Britain. Less than half the number of workplaces covered by existing laws were visited by health inspectors in 1975, with the total number of prosecutions for job safety violations being 2,000, and with the average fine imposed, often for conditions which could lead to the death or crippling injury of the worker concerned, being £40 — the price of an expense account luncheon.[29]

c. Cancer, determined in the overwhelming majority of cases by environmental conditions,[30] with individuals living in industrial working class neighbourhoods facing a much greater risk of dying of cancer than those who live in residential areas. All these are examples of the damage, caused by the economic and political environment, that brings about a demand for the expansion of health services.

4. *Control over the process of production*, i.e. workers' control. This demand has emerged in all sectors of economic and social activity in Britain (and in Continental Europe), including the health sector. Witness, for example, the demand by most of the unions in the health sector — from the National Union of Public Employees (NUPE) to the Confederation of Health Services Employees (COHSE) — for including employee (besides physician) representation on the RHAs and AHAs.[31]

5. *Public ownership of the means of production*, which has led large sectors of the Labour Movement to resist strongly any moves to denationalize presently nationalized sectors (like the coalmines or the NHS) or to abandon the famous Clause 4 of the Labour Party Constitution, committing that party to the nationalization of the means of production.

Thus, there is continuous pressure from the Labour Movement to expand social (including health) expenditures, as well as to change the pattern of control of such expenditures. This pressure, in turn, determines a series of responses from the capitalist class and the state that explain both the growth of these expenditures and the nature of that growth. It is important to stress that these responses always take place within the context of the primary function of the state, which is to ensure the process of capital accumulation. Because of this, let me focus now on the specific needs and requirements that that process determines.

The Growing Needs of the Process of Capital Accumulation

From Adam Smith to Marx, there has been agreement that the primary function of the state in capitalist society is to defend, support and encourage capital accumulation, i.e., to stimulate and strengthen the economy, upon whose health (or lack of it) everything else is assumed to depend. And a primary characteristic of that process of capital accumulation is, as indicated earlier, its concentration. Indeed, insurance, banking, manufacture, and other sectors of economic life are in the hands of an increasingly small number of corporations that, for the most part, control the market in each sector. Professor Florence, for example, has documented the growing concentration of industry, finding that less than 1% of all companies received 55% of total company income in 1951.[32] Just four years later, that 1% was receiving 61% of this income. Actually, the top 1% of British companies also monopolized 40% of the business of all concerns in private enterprise.[33]

The consequences of this concentration are many, but among them, the most important is the type of technology and industrial development demanded by, and intended primarily to serve the needs of, that concentration. And flowing from that economic concentration and its accompanying type of technological and industrial development are the following characteristics:

1. *A division of labour, with a continuous demand for specialization* that fragments the process of production of both goods and services. That division of labour and specialization expands to include all areas of economic and social activity, and aims, as Braverman[34] and Margolies[35] have shown, at optimizing the pattern of control that owners and managers have over the process of production and over the producers themselves. And that process of further division of labour and specialization

a. establishes a hierarchical order that complements and is based on the class structure and class relations of our societies, and

b. requires an increasing need for state intervention to both produce — via education and research — and allocate — via licensing and regulation — this division of labour.

Similarly in medicine, we find an increased division of labour and specialization aimed at optimizing the pattern of control of the process of production in medicine by the corporate class and the professions, and within them, particularly, by the academically based consultants. An order of authority and hierarchy is established that is determined primarily in the sphere of class relations. And here let me stress two essential points that I believe have escaped most social analysts of medicine.

The first one is that the primary controllers and managers of medicine are not the professionals but rather the controllers and managers of Capital. Indeed, as Susser[36] has written, the concept of health and even the nature of medical practice has continuously changed and has been redefined according to the needs of the capitalist modes and relations of production. The medical profession intervenes in that redefinition but *a posteriori*, i.e., they administer and influence but do not create the nature of medicine. For example, abortion on demand was recently considered to be medically acceptable and advisable in spite of the clear opposition of the medical profession. And that change in therapeutic 'vision' was the societal result of the need as perceived by the established centres of power to respond to an increasingly militant feminist movement and to the population policies perceived to be most convenient at that time.

The second point worth underlining is that, contrary to what most social theorists say, specialization in medicine is the result of the need created not by industrialization but rather by capital accumulation and its concomitant class relations. Ivan Illich[37] and A. Cochrane,[38] for example, consider the division of labour in medicine to be the result of the needs of industrialized and 'scientific' Flexnerian medicine. They assume that technology in medicine is a primary explanatory factor for the current medical division of labour which, in turn, determines the distribution of functions and responsibilities. Contrary to this interpretation, I believe that technology and 'scientific' medicine merely strengthen and legitimize a hierarchy and distribution of authority that is *already there*, and that is primarily, although not exclusively, a result of a distribution of power in Britain along class and sex (and, I might add, racial) lines.

Let me illustrate this with an analysis of the responsibilities that the members of the health team have. Within the health team, we find a well-defined hierarchical order with the physician, most often a man of upper-middle class extraction, at the top; below him, the supportive nurses, most often women with lower-middle class backgrounds; and at the bottom, under both of them, we find the attendants and auxiliaries, the service workers, who most frequently are women of working class backgrounds.

According to Illich and other theorists of industrialism, what primarily explains this hierarchy is the different degrees of control over the technological knowledge necessary for the provision of industrialized medicine. But past and present experience shows that (1) the responsibilities that the different members of the team have are due primarily to their class backgrounds and sex roles, and only secondarily, very secondarily indeed, to their technological knowledge; and (2) this technological knowledge, far from causing the cleavage and hierarchy among these members, merely reinforces that hierarchy. In that respect, the acquisition of such knowledge — via education and training — is, as Simpson and Robson have documented,[39] the mere legitimation of that class and sex hierarchical distribution of power and responsibilities.

The 'scientific revolution' in medicine and the creation of scientific medicine further strengthened, but did not create, that class distribution of responsibilities within the health sector; they already existed. Indeed, to assume, as Illich does, that the distribution of responsibilities in medicine is due to its industrialization is to confuse symptoms with causes. It is primarily the class structure and the class relations of our society that determine that distribution.

A last note worth underlining is the effect that this division of labour and specialization has in establishing barriers to working class solidarity. The demands for higher productivity and higher specialization, which usually appear in times of social and economic crises — such as in today's Britain — can also be perceived as part of a strategy for dividing the threatening labour force. As a leading trade unionist in the health sector in Britain said recently, 'By dividing health workers into a multiplicity of sections and grades, the management tries to lead them to believe that they have no common interests and that indeed their interests are opposed'.[40] Actually, it is not uncommon in the hospitals of the NHS to find separate dining rooms for the different staff groupings. In St. Bartholomew's Hospital in London, for example, there are no less than five.[41]

To sum up, the concentration of economic and (as we will see later) political power, determines a type of technological development in all sectors of social life — including medicine — which increasingly strengthens and reinforces the hierarchicalization of our population, and which reproduces the class structure of capitalist societies. For that division of labour to take place, however, there is an increasing need for state intervention both to produce — via education and research — and allocate — via licensing and regulation — this division of labour in medicine. That specialization strengthens the hierarchical structure that is basically determined in the sphere of class relations. Indeed, as we have seen in Part I, that specialization is closely correlated with the class forces both within and outside the health sector. At the top, we find the private, part-time consultant based in the teaching hospitals and at the bottom, the community health services, with general practice falling in between. Reflecting this set of priorities, Table 7.7 shows the clear differences in expenditure in the various branches of the

TABLE 7.7 *Health Services as a Proportion of Total Cost of the NHS, 1950–1972*

Year	*Hospital*[(1)] *Services* %		*Pharma-ceutical Services* %		*General*[(2)] *Medical Services* %		*Local Health Authority Services* %	
1950	54.9		8.4		11.7		7.8	
1951	56.0		9.8		11.0		8.4	
1952	56.0		9.8		11.1		8.4	
1953	55.3		9.5		10.8		8.9	
1954	56.4		9.3		10.6		9.2	
1955	57.3		9.6		10.2		8.7	
1956	57.6		9.8		10.0		8.6	
1957	57.0		9.7		10.3		8.7	
1958	58.0		10.0		10.3		8.9	
1959	57.4		10.1		9.7		9.3	
1960	56.4		10.1		9.8		9.0	
1961	56.8		9.8		9.0		9.3	
1962	59.0		9.7		8.5		9.7	
1963	60.1		10.1		8.3		9.9	
1964	60.5		10.2		7.9		10.0	
1965	60.5		11.1		7.8		10.2	
1966	60.9		11.2		7.5		10.2	
1967	59.9		10.6		7.9		10.7	
1968	60.0		10.2		7.9		10.6	
1969(3)	61.2	63.1	10.1	10.4	7.8	8.0	10.4	7.4
1970		64.2		10.0		8.3		7.0
1971		65.5		9.8		8.1		6.9
1972		66.0		9.7		7.9		6.8
1973		66.2		9.4		7.4		6.6
1974(3)		67.0		9.0		6.5		(3)

(1) Expenditure has been adjusted to include, for the appropriate year, any areas of remuneration subsequently granted.
(2) Includes grants, central administration and items such as laboratory, vaccine and research costs not falling within the finance of any one service.
(3) Change in definition of NHS – certain local authority services transferred from NHS to Social Services.
Source: 'The Cost of NHS', OHE Information Sheet, No. 29, London, July (1976).

NHS. We find that the great majority of the expenditures of the NHS have gone to hospitals — the workshop for the consultants — and, moreover, that these expenditures, both in absolute amounts as well as in percentages, have grown since the NHS was established. Conversely, the percentage of expenditures for general practitioners' services and for community health services (operated by the local authorities) have been relatively small and, for the most part, have been declining.

An order of priorities is established in which hospitals have priority over general practice services, and both have priority over community health services (or public health services). And paraphrasing George Orwell, within hospitals 'some are more equal than others'. In analysing the evolution of the pattern of expenditures of the NHS, we can see that during the period 1963-1969 (while there were no major attempts to develop the community health services), there was a dramatic increase in the percentage of capital expenditure going to teaching, acute hospitals (from 13.9 to 19.6%), with, incidentally, 37% of this growth going to the 'cream' of the teaching hospitals — the ones in the London area.[42] Thus, a hierarchy is established in which teaching hospitals have priority over non-teaching hospitals with respect to the allocation of resources, and in spite of the fact that according to the few studies that have been conducted, the latter had a heavier load of patients that were more ill than the former. Perhaps one should conjecture as a possible explanation of this inequity that the non-teaching hospitals also had more patients from working class backgrounds and included more of the elderly than those patients in teaching hospitals who were customarily from the middle class and were younger.[43]

And within the non-teaching hospitals a pattern of expenditures is established whereby the order of priorities for those needing care is as follows: the acutely ill, the chronically ill, the geriatric patient, the

TABLE 7.8 *Cost Per Inpatient Week for Selected Services in Different Types of NHS Hospitals in England, 1969/70 (In £)*

	Acute, Non-Teaching, Over 100 Beds	*Long-Stay, Geriatric & Chronic Sick*	*Mental Illness*	*Mental Handicap*
Net Total Cost	55.70	22.50	17.63	14.96
Medical Staff	3.10	0.46	0.81	0.39
Nursing Staff	13.67	9.55	6.26	5.28
Domestic Staff	2.77	1.67	0.60	0.44
Catering	6.07	2.81	2.64	2.23
Laundry	1.20	0.74	0.40	0.46
Power, Heat & Light	1.88	1.21	0.88	0.78
General Cleaning	0.55	0.32	0.15	0.13

Source: J. Tudor Hart, 'A New Kind of Doctor', *International Journal of Health Services* (in process).

mental patient, and the mentally-handicapped patient, with the amount of expenditures being in declining order. It is worth mentioning that these inequities in resources and expenditures among the different types of hospitals affect all forms of services, i.e., not only medical staff salaries, but also other non-medical services such as laundry, general cleaning, catering, and others (see Table 7.8).

It is worth stressing that it is precisely this pattern of class and professional controls that determines the pattern of priorities within the NHS and its concomitant pattern of expenditures, marked by a never-ending expansion of the very costly and highly technological, hospital-based type of care for the acutely ill patient.

2. *An invasion of all spheres of social life by corporate capital and its process of industrialization*, causing dislocation, diswelfare and insecurity, that state intervention, through social services (including medical services), is supposed, in turn, to mitigate. The most important example, of course, is the alienation that the industrialized process of production causes in the working population — an alienation that reflects itself, in large degree, in psychosomatic conditions (the most frequent problem in primary medical care in Britain and other capitalist developed countries) and that medicine is expected to care for and cure.

Similarly, occupational disease — which, as indicated before, has been convincingly defined by some as 'the new plague' of developed societies — and environmental damage are, for the most part, also corporately caused; but, according to bourgeois ideology, individually cured through medical intervention. In summary, the concentration of economic power and its consequent process of industrialization creates dislocation and diswelfare which, in turn, determine and require the growth of state services, including medicine. Thus, medicine is assigned an impossible task — that of taking care of, solving, and administering the disease, unease, and diswelfare created by the process of production and consumption in capitalism; or in other words, solving the unsolvable. In that respect, the great concern about the *apparent ineffectiveness of medicine* in solving our health problems seems to ignore the fact that the main function of medicine in present-day capitalism is not to solve or cure, but to take care of and administer the diswelfare that is created by the social relations of production. In other words, the much-heralded crisis of effectiveness of the Western system of medicine, including the British one, is a result of the inability of medicine to deal with and even change the economic and social forces that determine most of the prevalent mortality and morbidity in the first place. Let me further add that the fact that medicine has not been effective in reducing mortality and morbidity does not mean it is not useful. Indeed, medicine not only takes care of this diswelfare, but most importantly, by creating the social consciousness that what is actually a collective and political problem — diswelfare — can be treated individually (via the medical intervention), medicine has a legitimation function in the capitalist system. Thus, it transforms what should be a collective response into an individual one. Medicine has a double function. On the one hand, it ameliorates and makes palatable the diswelfare created in the sphere of production and consumption. Therefore, it has been incorporated into the realm of demands made by the working population to reduce the damage that is imposed on our population. On the other hand, medicine also has a legitimation function, i.e., to make people believe that what is politically and collectively caused can be individually and therapeutically cured. These two functions explain, to a large degree, the growth of medicine and its ineffectiveness.

TABLE 7.9 *Funds Allocated to Hospital Services by Region, per Resident: England, 1963*

Region	*Allocation* (£) *per Resident*
Newcastle	8.9
Leeds	9.3
Sheffield	7.6
East Anglia	7.7
N.W. Met.	9.4
N.E. Met.	10.7
S.E. Met.	10.7
S.W. Met.	11.7
Oxford	9.4
South-West	10.4
Birmingham	8.4
Manchester	8.8
Liverpool	10.4
Wessex	10.1
Welsh	9.8

Source: General Register Office, 1963.

3. *An increased dislocation of personal and social life*, accompanied by the steady breaking down of the social systems of support (e.g., the family) which need to be replaced by tax-supported services (e.g., nursing homes and day care centres), in order to facilitate the individual's participation in the process of production.

4. *An increased concentration of resources in urban areas*, required for the realization of capital, with deployment of resources into these urban spaces. This process of urbanization necessitates a growth in the allocative functions of the state (e.g., land-use legislation and city planning), as well as of productive functions (e.g., roads and sanitation), so as to support, guide, and direct that process in a way that is responsive to the needs of capital accumulation.[44]

TABLE 7.10 *Distribution of Distinction Awards to Consultants by British Hospital Regions, 1966**

	The number of award holders in each region expressed as a percentage of the total number of consultants in each region				
Region	*Percentage of award holders in region*	*A plus £4,885 (87)*	*A £3,700 (275)*	*B £2,175 (825)*	*C £925 (1649)*
Liverpool	25.4	0.6	2.4	8.3	14.1
Birmingham	25.7	0.6	2.8	7.3	15.0
Manchester	25.9	0.4	2.6	7.3	15.5
Sheffield	26.4	0.3	2.8	7.3	15.9
Leeds	27.1	0.6	3.5	8.4	14.7
Wales	28.2	0.9	3.5	7.7	16.2
Wessex	28.6	0.3	1.9	8.8	17.6
Newcastle	29.9	0.5	2.3	9.1	18.0
South Western	30.3	0.6	2.6	8.2	19.0
East Anglia	30.6	0.7	3.7	9.2	17.0
Oxford	31.5	2.2	2.2	8.8	18.2
All Metrop. Regions	36.8	1.4	3.7	10.7	21.0
England and Wales	31.04	0.95	3.01	9.03	18.05
Scotland	32.13	0.97	3.00	9.36	18.80

*Rates payable from 1/10/66. Honorary consultants are included. Consultants with appointments in more than one region are included in each.

Sources: Ministry of Health *Annual Report, 1966* (Cmnd. 3326) July (1967), pp. 177 and 45; Scottish Home and Health Department, *Health and Welfare Services in Scotland, 1966* (Cmnd. 3337) August (1967), p. 39.

That accumulation of resources also occurs in medicine. Health resources tend to be based in the urbanized, wealthiest areas, following a pattern of expenditures which, as Tudor Hart has noted, can be described as following *the inverse care law*, i.e., the greater the need for services, the lower the expenditures on such services.[45] To illustrate this point, Table 7.9 shows the funds allocated to hospital services, per resident, for 1963. And we can see how the more urbanized and wealthy areas, primarily the South East and the South West, are those with a higher allocation per resident. The consultants in the hospital services in the South and East regions — the wealthiest in the U.K. —

TABLE 7.11 *Proportionate Contribution Made to Junior Staffing of Hospitals by Doctors From Overseas, 1967*

Hospital region	*Proportion of total staff in Junior Grades (excluding provisionally registered house officers) represented by doctors not born in Great Britain (%)*
England and Wales	46.1
Newcastle	57.1
Leeds	57.1
Sheffield	57.1
Manchester	53.8
Birmingham	51.4
East Anglia	48.5
Oxford	47.0
Wales	42.2
Metropolitan (4 regions)	41.9
Liverpool	39.6
South Western	36.3
Wessex	33.5
Scotland	19.9
Northern	27.3
South Eastern	25.3
Western	19.1
North Eastern	14.5
Eastern	10.4
Great Britain	42.8

Source: Based on Table 5 in Ministry of Health, *Report of the Joint Working Party on the Medical Staffing Structure in the Hospital Service*, p. 88.

received a higher number of merit awards than in the other regions, as shown in Table 7.10. Few rewards, awards, and expenditures go to the northern part of England, however, where the dependency of hospital staff on foreign doctors, depicted in Table 7.11, is greatest.

TABLE 7.12 *Average List Size of Principal General Medical Practitioners by Region, with Extremes within Each Region, 1973*

Region		*List Size*	*Percentage variation from national average*
North			
Worst	Hartlepool	2951	+23.0
Best	Westmoorland	1839	–23.3
Yorkshire and Humberside			
Worst	Rotherham	2832	+18.0
Best	Yorks, East Riding	2169	–9.5
East Midlands			
Worst	Northampton	2656	+10.7
Best	Lincs. (Kesteven)	2210	–7.8
East Anglia			
Worst	Hunts & Peterborough	2628	+9.5
Best	Suffolk East	2158	–10.0
South East			
Worst	Beds. and Luton	2269	–5.4
Best	Bournemouth	2048	–14.5
South West			
Worst	Wiltshire	2361	–1.5
Best	Isles of Scilly	1100	–54.1
West Midlands			
Worst	Wolverhampton	2738	+14.1
Best	Herefordshire	1926	–19.6
North West			
Worst	St. Helens	2858	+19.1
Best	Birkenhead	2160	–9.9
Wales			
Worst	Glamorgan	2416	+0.7
Best	Merionethshire	1574	–34.4
England and Wales			
Worst	Hartlepool	2951	+23.0
Best	Isles of Scilly	1100	–54.1
Average		2398	–

Source: Derived from Ministry of Health, *Annual Report*; and B. Buxton, *Health and Inequality*, London, Open University Press (1976).

Similarly, as shown in Table 7.12 for *general practitioners' services*, we find that there are more GPs per population, and therefore fewer people per GP, in the South and East regions than in the North and West regions,[46,47] with a more favourable age distribution of the GPs working in the former than in the latter areas.[48] As Tudor Hart has indicated, we also find that the dependency on foreign graduates is higher in the North and West regions than in the South and East.

Regarding *community health services*, we find a similar pattern of regional inequity. Coates and Rawstron have shown, for example, that there are more school medical services, per child, in counties and boroughs of the South and East, than in the North and West regions.[49]

FIGURE 7.1 *The Relationship Among Different Forces Towards The Urbanization of Medicine*

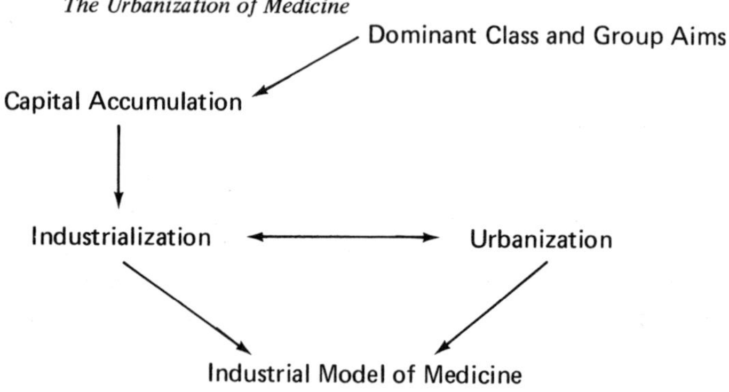

(1) Flexnerian Scientific Medicine
(2) Hospital-Oriented Specialization
(3) White Collarization and Urbanization of Medical Students
(4) Technologicalization of Medicine

DISTRIBUTION OF RESOURCES
Towards Urban and Wealthy Areas
Towards Hospital-Based Specialties
Away from Rural and Poor Areas
Away from Ambulatory Care

To sum up, then, the economic concentration typical of the present stage of capitalism in Britain — and in all developed capitalist countries — determines (1) an invasion by corporate capital of all spheres of economic, social, and even private life, and (2) a specific type of technological development and industrialization that requires increased state intervention to (a) stimulate and facilitate that concentration, and (b) rectify the dislocation of general well-being created by that concentration.

Moreover, this process of economic concentration and its concomitant industrialization determines a model of production and distribution in medicine that reproduces the characteristics of the overall process of economic production and distribution, i.e., specialization, concentration, a technical orientation in medicine, and urbanization. This set of relationships is graphically presented in Figure 7.1.

THE MEANING OF THE 'NEW' INEQUITIES

There is presently a strong tendency in medical care literature to dismiss and consider irrelevant the whole concept of social class as a determinant of power in the production of resources and as a determinant of differentials in the consumption of those resources. Indeed, in the realm of consumption, it is believed that as a result of welfare state measures, such differentials by class have dramatically diminished and have been superseded by persisting or newly created inequalities, such as imbalances by region or type of care. Cochrane, for example, in an influential volume on the British National Health Service,[50] indicates that, because of the NHS, differences in the consumption of medical care by social class have virtually disappeared in Great Britain. And he takes Titmuss and Tudor Hart to task for their undue concern about class inequities and irregularities; because, according to him, there are far more important inequities to worry about.[51] Actually, in what is held to be the most thorough and best known analysis of equity of health services in the U.K., the U.S. and Sweden, social class as a cause of cleavage and of differential consumption is neither considered, nor even mentioned.[52]

What these theorists do not realize, however, is that these 'new' inequities do represent and reflect social class differentials. In that respect, social class, far from having been transcended as a valid category for explaining the world of production and consumption, remains the axis and the centre of that explanation. Indeed, as I explained in the previous section, in order to explain these 'new' inequities, we have to first understand the class structure and the class relations of today's Britain.

Let us examine, for example, the regional inequities that I just described in the distribution of resources in the NHS. These inequities are not independent from either the class structure or the class relations of today's Britain. Of the former, Coates and Rawstron, in a survey of regional distribution of medical services,[53] concluded that the higher the proportion of persons in socio-economic group I (employers, managers, and professional workers) in the region, the higher the proportion of dentists (and, Coates and Rawstron add, of the overall volume of treatment carried out and paid for by the National Health Service) in that region. And conversely, the higher the proportion of persons in socio-economic group III (mainly skilled and semi-skilled manual workers), the lower the proportion of dentists and general practice services. Actually, if we analyse the inter-regional differences in availability of consultants and general practitioners' services in the NHS, we see that those regions with a higher percentage of working class residents (and primarily of the low-income stratum within it) are also those with the lower availability of resources.[54] And even within each service and within the same region, the nature of resources depended very much on the social class of the residents in the communities. For example, Cartwright and Marshall found that, in working class areas, 80% of the GPs' surgery buildings were built before 1900, and only 5% were built since the war, while in middle class areas and regions the proportions were 50% and 25% respectively.[55]

Similarly, in terms of the ordering of priorities on the basis of type of care, we have seen how the division of labour and hierarchicalization within medicine — with the acute part-time consultant at the teaching hospital at the top and, at the bottom, the public health worker — is not independent from the overall hierarchicalization of British class society. And, as I have indicated before, the latter is what determines the former, and not vice versa.

Therefore, it is this class structure that determines these new inequities and imbalances by region and type of care. And the evolution and shifts in these inequities, as indicated in the previous section, are explained by the state of class relations in Britain, i.e., by the social demands of Labour and the social needs of Capital. In that respect, the tendency towards further specialization, hierarchicalization, urbanization and hospital-oriented medicine — tendencies determined by the social needs of Capital — is balanced by a demand on the part of the working class to correct those imbalances and redistribute resources in a more equitable way.

The NHS, which, as indicated before, represented a tremendous victory for the working class, has had an impact on the overall availability of resources, improving both their accessibility and distribution. For example, the percentage of the British population living in underdoctored areas declined very dramatically in the early years of the NHS. In England and Wales, the percentage of people living in underdoctored areas was reduced from 52% in 1952, to 17% in 1961 (with the primary reductions taking place in South Wales, Northern England, and the Midlands).[56] But that demand by the working population is in continuous conflict with the demand of Capital, with its inherent tendency towards specialization, technologicalization, concentration, and urbanization, and with its subsequent deployment of resources towards highly specialized, urban and hospital-oriented services. The conflict between these forces, given by the level of class relations at the time and the relative dominance of one set of demands over the other, determines whatever changes in the distribution of resources take place. In that respect, the redistribution effort that came about at the beginning of the NHS has been reversed, and since 1961 there has been an increase in the percentage of people living in underdoctored areas — from 17% in 1961, to 34% in 1967.[57] And that reversal was due to the declining number of medical graduates (resulting from the control of the apparatus of production of physicians by academic medicine, which — as shown in Part I — was strengthened with the NHS) and increasing deployment to the hospital services.[58] The redistribution of GPs after the founding of the NHS was due to the redeployment of an abundant GP pool. To the degree that the dominance by the 'cream' of the profession — the academic London-based consultants — over the organs of production and distribution of human resources increased, that dominance strengthened the trend towards urbanization and hospitalization inherent in the capitalist system, reversing the trend towards redistribution that the NHS had created. Since then, the response to correct this situation has been to provide economic incentives to encourage

GPs to practise in underdoctored areas. The other alternative — that of changing the pattern of class and academically-based dominance and control over the organs of production and distribution of those resources, with actual democratization in the apparatus of production and allocation of resources in the NHS — has not even been considered. And while it is likely that in the future, successful pressure will be applied to dilute the professional dominance of the NHS, it is highly unlikely that the pattern of *class* control — different from professional control — will change. Indeed, it would be considered 'unnatural' within the capitalist system. Let us now, in Part III, analyse how that pattern of social class and professional dominance appears and is replicated in the NHS.

NOTES

1 See Navarro, 'Social Class, Political Power and the State and their Implications in Medicine', *op. cit.*

2 Cited in H. Frankel, *Capitalist Society and Modern Sociology*, Surrey, Lawrence and Wishart (1970), p. 77.

3 *The Economist* (January 15, 1966).

4 *Ibid.*

5 For a fascinating debate on the historical origins of the British upper class, see P. Anderson *op. cit.*; T. Nairn, 'The British Political Elite', *New Left Review*, 23 (1964); and Thompson, 'The Peculiarities of the English', in Miliband and Saville, *op. cit.*, p. 311.

6 J. Urry and J. Wakeford (eds.), *Power in Britain: Sociological Readings*, London, Heinemann (1973).

7 Frankel, *op. cit.*, p. 213.

8 In this presentation of classes and the strata within classes, I have very closely followed Chapter 2, 'Economic Elites and Dominant Classes', in R. Miliband, *The State in Capitalist Society*, London, Weidenfeld and Nicolson (1970), pp. 23-48.

9 A. Levinson, *The Working Class Majority*, New York, Coward, McCann, and Geoghegan, Inc. (1974).

10 Frankel, *op. cit.*

11 Consumption of income is considered an attribute but not a determinant of class.

12 M.A. Simpson, *Medical Education: A Critical Approach*, London, Butterworths (1972), p. 39.

13 Robson, *op cit.*

14 Simpson, *op. cit.*, p. 39.

15 *Evidence of the Royal College of Surgeons to the Royal Commission on Doctors' and Dentists' Remuneration,* London, Her Majesty's Stationery Office (1958).

16 See 'Trends of Mobility and Educational Opportunity', in Westergaard and Resler, *op. cit.*, pp. 314-342.

17 Incidentally, it is worth clarifying here what is a rather prevalent confusion — i.e., the fact that more than half of the GNP (52.1%) goes towards public expenditure is usually interpreted as meaning that capitalism has been transcended and that Britain has a mixed economy. But what establishes whether an economy is capitalist or socialist is the ownership of the means of production, which, in Britain, is predominantly in private hands. Moreover, even in those sections of the means of production that are publicly owned (40% of British land is publicly owned), the state is hopelessly mortgaged, through what is known as the National Debt, to private and international banks. In 1975, this National Debt was nearly £30,000 million — considerably more than what the state owns. See Frankel, *op. cit.*

18 10% of all U.K. manufacturing industry output is purchased by the central government alone. T. Chester, 'Public Money in the Private Sector', *National Westminster Bank Review*, (May 1973), p. 24.

19 I. Gough, 'State Expenditure in Advanced Capitalism', *New Left Review*, 92 (1975), p. 63.

20 O.E.C.D., *Expenditure Trends in O.E.C.D. Countries, 1960-1980* (1972), Table 16, p. 19.

21 Allocative policies are those state policies aimed at influencing, guiding, or even directing the allocation of resources, via laws and regulations. Productive policies are the state policies whereby the state directly participates in the production of resources. See Part III of this volume.

22 D. Widgery, 'Unions and Strikes in the National Health Service in the United Kingdom', *International Journal of Health Services*, 6(2) (1976), p. 301.

23 Quoted in *Whose Priorities?*, London, Radical Statistics Health Group (1976), p. 14.

24 Westergaard and Resler, *op. cit.*

25 A. Gamble and P. Walton, *Capitalism in Crisis: Inflation and the State,* New York, Macmillan (1976), p. 7.

26 S.S. Lewis, 'Nurses and Trade Unions in Britain', *International Journal of Health Serives*, 6(4) (1976), p. 641.

27 B. Fine and L. Harris have shown that the actual rate of unemployment is far higher for certain sectors of industry such as textiles and clothing where low-paid women workers — the type of workers we find in health services — predominate.

B. Fine and L. Harris, 'The British Economy: May 1975 – January 1976', *Bulletin of the Conference of Socialist Economists*, V (October 1976), p. 1.

28 P. Kinnersly, *The Hazards of Work*, London, Pluto Press (1973); and H. Grundwald, 'Safety and Health at Work', *Comment*, 2(21) (1973).

29 J. Robson, 'History and the Robens Report', *Medicine in Society*, 1(3) (1974), p. 10.

30 J. Cairns, 'The Cancer Problem', *Scientific American*, 233 (1975); and E.C. Hammond, 'Epidemiologic Basis for Cancer Prevention'. *Cancer*, 33(6) (1974).

31 M. Taylor, 'NHS Reorganization, An Opportunity for Democratic Control?' in M. Barrett Brown and K. Coates (eds.), *Trade Union Register, 3*, London, Spokesman Books (1973).

32 P. Florence, *Ownership, Control and Success of Large Companies: An Analysis of English Industrial Structure and Policy, 1936-1951*, London, Sweet and Maxwell (1961).

33 Frankel, *op. cit.*, p. 93.

34 H. Braverman, *Labour and Monopoly Capital*, New York, Monthly Review Press (1974).

35 S.A. Margolies, 'What Do Bosses Do? The Origins and Functions of Hierarchy in Capitalist Production', *The Review of Radical Political Economics*, 6(2) (1974), pp. 60-112.

36 M. Susser, 'Ethical Components in the Definition of Health', *International Journal of Health Services*, 4(3) (1974), pp. 539-548.

37 I. Illich, *Medical Nemesis: The Expropriation of Health*, London, Calder and Boyars (1975).

38 A. Cochrane, *Effectiveness and Efficiency: Random Reflections on Health Services*, London, Nuffield Provincial Hospitals Trust (1972).

39 Simpson, *op. cit.*, and Robson, 'The NHS Company, Inc.? The Social Consequence of the Professional Dominance in the National Health Service', *op. cit.*

40 'The Way Forward for Health Workers', *Needle*, 12 (1972).

41 M. Taylor, 'Creating A Health Workers' Democracy', in Brown and Coates, *op. cit.*, p. 169.

42 N. Bosanquet, 'Inequalities in the Health Service', *New Society*, 17(450) (1971) p. 809.

43 J.A.H. Lee, S.L. Morrison and J.M. Morris, 'Fatality from Three Common Regional Conditions in Teaching and Non-Teaching Hospitals', *The Lancet* (October 19, 1957), p. 785.

44 D. Harvey, *Social Justice and the City*, London, Edward Arnold Publishers, Ltd. (1973): and M. Castells, *The Urban Question*, London, Edward Arnold Publishers, Ltd. (1977).

45 J. Tudor Hart, 'The Inverse Care Law', *The Lancet*, i(7696) (1971), p. 405.

46 Except Wales, where the majority of GPs come from the same area. 72% of the GPs working in Wales are from Wales. Tudor Hart, 'The Inverse Care Law', *op. cit.*, p. 409.

47 B. Coates and E. Rawstron, *Regional Variations in Britain*, London, B.T. Batsford (1971).

48 D. Irvine and M. Jefferys, 'BMA Planning Unit Survey of General Practice, 1969', *British Medical Journal* (November 4, 1971), p. 535.

49 Coates and Rawstron, *op. cit.*, p. 193.

50 Cochrane, *op. cit.*, p. 70.

51 *Ibid.*

52 O. Anderson, *op. cit.*

53 Coates and Rawstron, *op. cit.*, p. 210.

54 A. Learmonth, 'Regional Disparities in the Health Sector', in Learmonth, *op. cit.*

55 A. Cartwright and R. Marshall, 'General Practice in 1963: Its Conditions, Contents and Satisfactions', *Medical Care*, 3(2) (April-June, 1965), pp. 69-87.

56 Coates and Rawstron, *op. cit.*, p. 192.

57 Tudor Hart, 'Inverse Care Law', *op. cit.*

58 J. Butler, *Family Doctors and Public Policy*, London, Routledge and Kegan Paul (1973), p. 10.

PART III

The Nature of State Intervention in the Health Sector in Great Britain

CHAPTER VIII

State Intervention in the NHS

INTRODUCTION

The literature on the nature of state intervention in the United Kingdom is, by now, extensive and varied. And in that literature the authors who, in my opinion, have contributed most to our understanding of the politics of the NHS are those who have used a 'power élite' paradigm as the basis for their evaluation of how and why the NHS took the form and shape that it did and that it does today.[1] The method of analysis flowing from this paradigm has been, first, to identify the groups and élites that assumedly play a dominant role in the NHS, such as the Royal Colleges, the BMA, and others; second, to analyse how that power is exercised and through which mechanisms, instruments, and bodies (e.g., General Medical Council); and third, to describe the nature of the benefits those groups obtain as a result of their intervention. It is worth stressing that the contribution of these authors to our understanding of the NHS has not been a small one. On the contrary, they have provided extremely important empirical information for the analysis of the NHS. The limitation of such 'power élite' interpretations is a result of their focus on the health sector (to the exclusion of consideration of forces outside that sector), together with their seeming unawareness of the concept of social class — factors which seriously curtail the explanatory value of their theories. Indeed, as I have indicated elsewhere, in order to understand the dynamics of the health sector and the behaviour of its actors, we have to be aware of the positions of these actors within the overall economic and political scheme of our societies, i.e., their class positions.[2] In this respect, the main weakness of the power élite theorists is their failure to recognize that those élites in the health sector are, in reality, segments of a dominant class and that, when considered in a systemic and not just a sectorial fashion, they are found to possess a high degree of cohesion and solidarity, with common interests and common purposes which far transcend their specific differences and disagreements. Consequently, those authors do not include in their analyses the non-actors and the non-decisions which may be far more important than the visible and intervening actors and the studied actual decisions. In other words, the not-so-competitive (as the 'power élite' theorists postulate) conflict among power groups or élites in Western societies for dominance and even control of the organs of the state takes place within the framework of a set of established class relations and within a well-defined capitalist structure, the maintenance and reproduction of which is the primary role of the state, the subject of the competition. This state role establishes a set of constraints for that competition (which I will detail later) that are of paramount importance in understanding the nature of the conflict and of the system. And again, as I will show later on, in that competition among groups and élites, the non-actors and non-decisions are as important as, if not more important than, the actors and decisions. In fact, both non-decisions and decisions respond to the dynamics of the British society — a society that I define as a capitalist society and that has a rationality of its own.[3]

A further weakness of the 'power élite' theories is that they define the main dynamic of the NHS as that of conflict resolution among different groups of actors and individuals whose *behaviour* and *motivation* determine the nature of the conflict. In that respect, such analysis runs the risk of viewing personalities and their individual motivations as the predominant forces in those conflicts.[4]

In order to correct this limitation, we have to understand the nature of the state within the class structure and class relations of British society. And only then, and within this broader context, can we study the distribution and composition of resources *within* the NHS — i.e., resulting from and a consequence of a pattern of class dominance, in which different groups, strata or élites of those classes have varying degrees of influence over the state.

Let us start, then, by defining what we mean by 'the state' in Britain. And in referring to the state, I include the executive and legislative branches of government as well as the state apparatus, i.e., the administrative bureaucracy, the judiciary, the army and the police. Also, it is important to clarify that I consider the state to be far more than the mere aggregate of those public institutions. Rather, it includes the set of relationships between and among those institutions, as well as with other ones that it guides and directs (such as the medical institutions). These relationships are aimed, as I will show later on in this section, at perpetuating the system of production and its concomitant class relations.[5] How does that aim materialize? First and foremost, through the reproduction of an economic system based on private ownership of the means of production, i.e., the capitalist economy. Let me further expand on this. The primary role of the state is to defend, support and encourage the capitalist economy upon whose health (or lack of it) everything else is assumed to depend. In other words, the primary function of a government, for example, is to give primacy to the interests of the economy as a whole, whose sanctity is considered to be above the interests of specific groups. Consider, for example, the dramatic cuts in social expenditure of both the Wilson and Callaghan governments — cuts made to save the troubled British economy. Let me quickly add that such policies are not a result of the malevolence of individuals or the manipulation of government by certain economic groups. Rather, these policies respond to a need perceived by those governments that the economy, whose smooth functioning is supposedly in our best interest, has to be straightened out before 'we can think of other matters'.

Needless to say, by 'the economy' is meant the capitalist economy, with the class structure and class relations that it subsumes and which I have previously described.[6]

How, then, does the state establish the conditions for the economy to operate? In many different ways, the most important of which are:

1. *The development of what is usually referred to as the infrastructure of production*, i.e. the development of those goods (e.g., roads, railways) and services (e.g., education and medical care) needed for the process of production and distribution in our economy and for the reproduction of the labour force. All of these goods and services have the characteristic that for only one individual or corporation to buy them would either be too costly or too risky (in the sense that making a profit would be too uncertain or that the possibilities of monopolizing their use would be very limited).[7]

2. *The legitimation and defence of the system through:*

a. the actual delivery of goods and services in response to different pressures mediated in the political process, of which the most important pressures are those generated by the conflict among classes. That provision of services is aimed (although not always successfully) at increasing the level of cohesion among classes and groups in a society and avoiding its disruption. Thus, for example, social legislation has been implemented historically at moments of labour unrest. As Henry Sigerist pointed out:

> Social-security legislation came in waves and followed a certain pattern; strong political parties representing the interests of the workers seemed a potential threat to the existing order, or at least to the traditional system of production, and an acute scare such as that created by the French Commune stirred Conservatives into action and social-security legislation was enacted. In England at the beginning of our century the second industrial revolution was very strongly felt. The Labour Party entered Parliament and from a two-party country, England developed into a three-party country. The Russian revolution of 1905 was suppressed to be sure, but seemed a dress rehearsal for other revolutions to follow. Social legislation was enacted not by the Socialists but by Lloyd George and Churchill.[8]

And as Harold Laski puts it:

> Social legislation is not the outcome of a rational and objective willing of the common good by all members of the community alike; it is the price paid for those legal principles which secure the predominance of the owners of property. It waxes and wanes in terms of their prosperity. It is a body of conscience offered to avert a decisive challenge to the principle by which their authority is maintained.[9]

b. the development, maintenance and stimulation of a value-generating system (such as the media and academic institutions), which sustains a system of values that, while appearing natural and commonsensical, are actually the values (e.g., individualism and competitiveness) most convenient to the survival of the economic system.

3. *The control over physical force*, to be used against internal and external threats against the system.

It is important to note that for the state to be able to establish conditions (1) and (2), it must be perceived, at least by the majority of the population, as being neutral, above classes, and serving common interests. The state's claim that it puts the condition of the economy first is legitimized on the grounds that it is necessary for the benefit of everyone in society. Thus calls for austerity and sacrifice are, in theory, calls for all, since everyone is in the same boat, i.e., the capitalist economy. As Offe has recently stated, 'The existence of a capitalist state presupposes the systematic denial of its nature as a capitalist state'.[10] It is only when that legitimation disintegrates and the supposedly classless nature of the state is called into question, that the state resorts to physical force, the third condition indicated above.

The Characteristics of the State

Those aims and functions of the state determine its non-neutrality. In other words, the state has a *class* character, and by this I mean that the state is subject to and the result of the influences of several classes, one of which — the capitalist class — is dominant. How does this dominance take place? I would postulate that it is through (1) the dependency of the state on the successful development of the economy, (2) the class origins and position of the top members of the organs of the state, (3) the ideology of the state, and (4) the structure of the state. Since I have explained each mechanism of influence elsewhere,[11] let me just briefly summarize the main points.

The Dependency of the State on the Successful Development of the Capitalist Economy

The size and scope of state activities are heavily dependent upon the successful development of the economy. State activities are funded through *taxes* on wages and profits, and through *credit*, increasing the national debt. And the mass of wages, profits and credit depend very much on the state of 'health' of the economy. Thus, when the latter suffers, the former shrink. Consequently, it is of paramount importance, for the expansion of the state, that the process of capital accumulation — the axle that keeps the economy moving — take place as unobstructedly and as smoothly as politically possible, since state resources depend on that capital accumulation. As Offe has indicated, 'accumulation . . . acts as the most powerful constraint criterion, but not necessarily as the content, of the policy-making process'.[12]

Of those state revenues, on which state expenditures depend, taxation has been the most important source. Data collected by Gough show that (1) from 1910 to 1970, taxation and trading surpluses rose roughly in line with expenditures, (2) alongside of this long-term growth in tax revenues there has also been a marked shift in the tax burden off corporations and onto households, and (3) since 1971 there have been dramatic trade deficits in the U.K., forcing the state to rely more heavily on credit, which increased the National Debt to a point precipitating 'the fiscal crisis of the British state'.[13] Thus, the present fiscal crisis of the state, with public expenditure outbalancing public revenues, is clearly related to the crisis of the British economy. The state is not an independent entity, but rather it is an intrinsic part of the capitalist system, in which the upper class rules. By defending, supporting and stimulating the economy on the one hand, and by being dependent on that economy on the other, the state acts as a pivotal force in the support and reproduction of the capitalist economy and its class relations. And, thus, its capitalist and class character.

The Class Origins of the Top Members of the Organs of the State

The class origins of the top members of the state organs in Britain have been well documented by, among others, Miliband,[14] Lupton and Wilson,[15] Guttsman,[16] and Fry.[17] Also, Roth[18] has shown the predominance of those of upper and upper-middle class backgrounds among MPs of both parties in Great Britain, with businessmen[19] (very rarely, if ever, businesswomen) representing one of the largest groups in the Cabinet from 1962 to 1967. That pattern of class origin is further accentuated in the top echelons of both parties, where the degree of social diversity is even smaller.

A similar situation appears in the upper strata of the civil service, where the majority come not only from private schools — which, as Peter Shore indicates, guarantee continuity in the ruling class[20] — but from the 'cream' of those schools, and then go on to the universities, where they receive the degree that finally legitimizes their right to rule. And in this apprenticeship for ruling, class origin is a determining factor. As was stated in the magazine of one of these universities, such institutions are considered to have a responsibility

> to civilize those who are born to great responsibilities, [and] the desire to be tender to the claims of loyal old members will, for a long time to come, continue to work to the benefit of the public schools rather than the obscurer grammar schools.[21]

The fact that the majority of the U.K. population did not attend private schools, but instead grammar, comprehensive and technical schools, exposes not only the class orientation of the British system of education, but also the function of that system, i.e., to legitimize the class divisions that exist in British society.

The top individuals in the government and civil service, and those in the upper echelons of finance and corporate capital, as well as of the professions, share a common class origin and have similar class positions. This fact is of paramount importance in understanding the nature and biases of state intervention both within and outside the health sector.

Here, it is necessary to stress that the determinant of the class composition of the state is the class nature of our society and not vice versa, i.e., what imparts a capitalist character to the state is its function, not its composition.[22] In a class society, it is just 'natural' that those in positions of power belong, for the most part, to the capitalist class — either by origin, association, or the sharing of beliefs. As Mandel has indicated, 'The capitalist state machine . . . possesses a hierarchical organization correspondent to the order of the capitalist society itself'.[23]

Here, let me add a note that I believe to be of great importance, and that concerns the key significance of the composition and ideology of the state. A recent debate between Poulantzas and Miliband has centred on the importance of that composition in defining, explaining, and understanding the nature of the state.[24] Poulantzas believes that what establishes a state as a capitalist state is its function, and not its composition. And I fully agree with that (and so, for that matter, does Miliband). But Poulantzas goes still further, maintaining that even if all members of the state, including its apparatus, were not members of the capitalist class by origin, i.e., if they were working class, that state would still be capitalist. But I find this position most deterministic. Indeed, the high degree of abstraction and generalization that French structuralists indulge in, and their disregard for empirical verification, leads them to miss the point of the story, i.e., that in not one of the capitalist societies (including the assumedly socialist society of Sweden) do members of the working class have more than a minimal role in the top corridors of the state and its apparatus.[25] And as long as those societies are capitalist, those 'on the top' of the state will be members of the capitalist class. Moreover, and as Miliband rightly points out, because of this failure to analyse (as French structuralists fail to do) the actual composition of the state and its meaning in policy formulation, they run the risk of blurring the distinction between a state run by fascists and one run by social democrats, since both are capitalist.

The Ideology of the State

Reflecting the class nature and class position of the state and its apparatus, we find that the top echelons of the civil service in Britain share an ideology that gives that apparatus an internal cohesiveness and logic of its own. It is the glue that keeps the pieces together. And that ideology is the one of the capitalist class. Indeed, 'success' in the civil service is related not so much to competence but primarily to the degree to which performance conforms to the tenets of those in power. It is utterly inconceivable, for example, that a person either rejecting or resisting the existing social order and its norms of thought and action could reach the top of the state apparatus. Indeed, as Mandel indicated:

> Convinced and active pacifists do not usually become generals, and it is absolutely certain that they do not become Chiefs of General Staff. To imagine that the bourgeois state apparatus could be used for a socialist transformation of capitalist society is as illusory as to suppose that an army could be dissolved with the aid of 'pacifist generals'.[26]

Similarly, it would be unimaginable that the top senior medical officers in Britain would believe in a classless society, with workers and community control of the health institutions.

Thus, there is a set of beliefs that members of the state apparatus must hold. One example is the belief required of them — and, for the most part, gladly held — regarding the primacy of the private sector. I am aware, of course, of the argument that those civil servants are merely reflecting the overall values of the society, and also that, for the most part, they are above specific economic or class interests. Indeed, as I indicated earlier, this appearance of being above class interests is of paramount importance in legitimizing both their conduct and the state apparatus. But empirical evidence shows that, for the most part, their ideas are the ideas of the powerful in society. And among these ideas, an important one is the primacy of the private sector and the need for strengthening the capitalist system, usually expressed in terms of 'strengthening the economy'. And the same applies, incidentally, to the series of advisory and consultant bodies set up by the state apparatus. Many studies have shown the predominance of members who uphold bourgeois positions in most advisory, policy-making bodies in the branches of the state.[27]

The Structure of the State and the Separation of Powers

A most important determinant of class power in capitalist societies is inherent in the structure of the state itself and its principle of separation of powers, in which the bodies responsible for the implementation of policies are separate from the bodies responsible for deciding and formulating those policies. This decision-making and formulation, however, is carried out indirectly through supposed representatives of the population seated in the executive and legislative branches of government — and not directly by the population itself. Thus, Western democracies are indirect democracies, and, we may add, incomplete democracies. Indeed, due to the skewed nature of political debate, political parties which question the basic assumption of the capitalist system are systematically hindered from participating in the electoral system and seriously handicapped from presenting their views in the marketplace of ideas, to the advantage of those parties which do accept the system.

Moreover, the indirect character of Western democracies is being increasingly strengthened by the remarkable shift of the power of political decision-making from the legislative to the executive branches of government and to the central administrative machinery, a shift which has left an indelible imprint on most Western parliamentarian and congressional systems. This shift of power from the legislative to the executive branch and to the state apparatus (primarily the central administration) is not independent of nor unrelated to the shift of the capitalist mode of production from competitive to monopolistic. Indeed, the increasing concentration of state policy within the executive branch and the central administration corresponds not so much to the requirements of the increasingly complex post-industrial societies, but rather to the increased centralization of economic power and its dominance over both the executive and administrative branches of government. I would postulate that the increased centralization of economic and management policies in the NHS (with the 1974 reorganization)[28] are a response to pressures on the state organs by the monopolistic segments to do something about the 'mess' in the health and social sectors.[29] Not infrequently, this process of centralization and increased bureaucratization further strengthens the tendency, inherent in the internal rationale of the capitalist system, to separate the governors from the governed and the administrators from those administered or, as Lenin indicated, to separate the state from society.[30]

Politics in bourgeois democracies, therefore, takes place in the realm of the politicians — the experts in the art of politicking — and not in people's everyday lives. As a recent powerful international commission on the study of Western democracies indicated, Western democracies work best when the citizenry is passive and somewhat apathetic, and when its input into the political process takes place only through a limited electoral system.[31] Thus, the implied, and I might add actual, function of the electoral system is to legitimize the political process rather than to secure the people's participation in their own governance. In consequence, as Wolfe has recently pointed out, the electoral aim is the replication of a political institution 'which claims primary responsibility for reproducing alienated politics, i.e., for maintaining a political system based upon the extraction and imposition of power from people'.[32] Not surprisingly then, and as part of the increased consciousness of the population and the intensification of class struggle, that process of legitimization is quickly losing its validity. In fact, a primary problem in Western societies is the political alienation of increased masses of the population from the political system. And Britain has not been an exception. A recent study by Crewe, Särlvik and Alt, which examined its voting patterns from 1964 to 1974, confirms the previous findings of other studies that indicated (1) that there has been an increased disenchantment among the electorate regarding the two-party system of Britain as measured by the level and strength of party identification, and (2) that this disenchantment is greater among the young, the working class, and the trade union communities. These authors conclude that the obvious outcome of that trend 'would be the destabilization of the party system in Britain'.[33] This disenchantment is even more accentuated at the local authorities' level where there has been a steady decline of the percentage of turnout since 1946, with less than 40% of the electorate at present voting.[34]

The Mechanisms of State Intervention in the NHS

Having described, however briefly, the aims, functions, and composition of the state, we are now in a better position to be able to explain the nature of state intervention in the NHS. It was indicated earlier, you may remember, that while finding the 'power élite' paradigm useful in explaining the nature of the influences and dominances in the NHS, I consider that usefulness to be seriously limited because of the failure of such an approach to consider (1) the class (besides the 'power élite') nature of those decisions and interventions, and (2) the non-decisions and non-actions in those interventions, which, as I indicated, are equally, if not more, important than the decisions and actions actually taken.

Let us begin, then, by somewhat arbitrarily dividing those interventions into two levels: the mechanisms of negative selection and of positive selection.[35]

Negative Selection Mechanisms

By negative selection, I mean that mode of intervention that excludes systematically and continually those strategies that conflict with the class nature of the capitalist society. This negative intervention takes place through (1) structural selective mechanisms, (2) ideological mechanisms, (3) decision-making mechanisms, and (4) repressive coercion mechanisms.[36]

Structural selective mechanisms. These mechanisms refer to the exclusion of alternatives that threaten the capitalist system, an exclusion that is inherent in the nature of the capitalist state. Offe mentions, for example, the constitutionally guaranteed right in all capitalist societies to private property, which excludes state conflict with that right and with the class nature that right determines. In fact, the overall priority given to property and capital accumulation explains why, when health and property conflict, the latter usually takes priority over the former. For example, the appalling lack of adequate legislation protecting the worker in most capitalist societies contrasts most dramatically with the large array of laws protecting private property and its owners. And the dramatic insufficiency of British occupational programmes already discussed in this text clearly indicates (1) the greater dominance that Capital has over the state, and (2) that workers' lives and safety are secondary to the most important aim of capital accumulation.

This structural negative selective mechanism also appears in the implied assumption that all health programmes and reforms have to take place within the set of class relations prevalent in capitalist societies. For example, Bevan's Labour Party strategy of implementing the NHS (a victory for the British working class) assumed an unalterability of class relations in Britain. Indeed, the creation of the NHS was seen as taking place within the structure of capitalist Britain of 1948, respecting the class distribution of power both outside and within the health sector. In fact, Bevan relied very heavily on the consultants (who clearly were of upper class extraction and position) to break the resistance of the general practitioners against the implementation of the NHS. The strategy of using the nationalization of the health sector to break with the class structure outside and within the health sector, as Lenin did in the Soviet Union, was not even considered.[37] Moreover, to reassure the medical profession in general and the consultants in particular, the latter were given dominant influence over the process of planning, regulation, and administration of the health sector.[38] Actually, these mechanisms of class reassurances operated, as I indicated before, also in other nationalized sectors. As Coates has indicated, the men chosen by the Labour Government in the 1940's to lead the nationalized industries were all members of the managerial and ownership class of the former private industries.[39]

Ideological mechanisms. These mechanisms ensure the exclusion from the realm of debate of ideologies that conflict with the system. In other words, it is not only programmes and policies, as indicated before, that are being excluded but, more importantly, conflicting ideologies are also automatically being excluded. This is clearly shown in the lack of attention to and the lack of research in areas that conflict with the requirements and needs of the capitalist system. Reflecting the bourgeois bias of the medical research establishment, for example, much priority is given to the assumedly individual causation of disease. One instance, among others, is that most research on heart disease — one of the main killers in society — has focused on diet, exercise and genetic inheritance. On the study of these aetiologies, millions of pounds, dollars, marks and francs have been spent. However, in a fifteen-year study of ageing, quoted in a most interesting report entitled *Work in America* prepared by a special task force to the Secretary of HEW of the U.S., it was found that the most important predictor of longevity was work satisfaction. Let me quote from the report:

> In an impressive 15-year study of aging, the strongest predictor of longevity was work satisfaction. The second best predictor was overall 'happiness' . . . Other factors are undoubtedly important — diet, exercise, medical care, and genetic inheritance. But research findings suggest that these factors may account for only about 25% of the risk factors in heart disease, the major cause of death. That is, if cholesterol, blood pressure, smoking, glucose level, serum uric acid, and so forth, were perfectly controlled, only about one-fourth of coronary heart disease could be controlled. Although research on this problem has not led to conclusive answers, it appears that work role, work conditions, and other social factors may contribute heavily to this 'unexplained' 75% of risk factors.[40]

But very few studies have been done either in the U.K. or in the U.S. to investigate these socio-political factors. Indeed, studies on such subjects as work satisfaction have a threatening potential to the actual controllers of the work process since, as Braverman has clearly shown, the nature of the capitalist process of production is what actually determines that alienating work. To change the latter requires questioning the former.[41]

Similarly, in the reorganization of the NHS in 1974, Draper and Smart have convincingly shown that certain issues, positions, and ideologies that were considered to be threatening to the pattern of dominance in the NHS were consistently excluded from the realm of debate and consideration by the research and consultative institutions.[42]

In all these examples, I have shown how the success of ideologies and ideologues depends primarily on whether or not they harmonize with the chorus of the powerful.

The exclusion of ideologies which question or threaten the basic assumptions of the capitalist system is a most prevalent mechanism of state intervention, i.e., the exclusion of any alternatives as unthinkable.

Decision-making mechanisms. The decision-making processes are weighted heavily in favour of certain groups and classes, and thus against certain others. For example, the mechanism of selection and appointment of members to the new regional and area health planing and administrative agencies in Britain[43] is conducive to the dominance over those bodies of individuals of the corporate and upper-middle classes — to the detriment of members of the lower-middle and working classes, as shown in previous sections.

Repressive coercion mechanisms. These mechanisms take place either through the use of direct force or, more importantly, by cutting (and thus nullifying) those programmes that may conflict with sources of power within the state organism (e.g., the cutting or neglecting of the occupational health programmes).

Positive Selection Mechanisms

By positive selection, I mean the type of state intervention that generates, stimulates, and determines a positive response favourable to overall capital accumulation, rather than a negative one that excludes anti-capitalist possibilities. Offe distinguishes between two types of intervention — allocative and productive.[44] In the former, the state regulates and co-ordinates the allocation of resources that have already been produced, while in the latter, the state becomes directly involved in the production of goods and services.

Allocative intervention policies. These policies are based on the authority of the state in influencing, guiding, and even directing the main activities of society, including the most important one, capital accumulation. The policies are put into effect primarily (although not exclusively) through laws that make certain behaviour mandatory and through regulations that make certain claims legal. Examples of the former in the health sector are laws requiring doctors to register contagious disease with the state health department, and employers to install protective devices to prevent industrial accidents, while an example of the latter is regulations determining that certain categories of people receive health insurance.[45] Both laws and regulations are determined and dictated in the world of politics. As Offe indicates, in allocative functions 'policy and politics are not differentiated'.[46] And, as such, those policies are determined by the different degrees of dominance of the branches of the state by pressure groups and fractions primarily within the dominant class.

Here, we have to ask ourselves an important question. How do we go about studying those allocative policies and their class character? The most frequently used method is to analyse how, in either specific government policies or in historical events, the different classes and their components relate *via interpersonal relationships* with the organs of the state and its intermediary institutions such as political parties, professional associations, etc.[47]

Let us proceed, then, to a description of the various mechanisms of allocation of human health resources in the NHS and the subsequent dominance of that body by class and professional interests. Let us start by asking who makes the decisions concerning the allocation of human health resources within the NHS, specifically decisions as to the different groups of MDs (consultants, registrars, GPs and public health physicians), and through what mechanisms.

1. *Consultants and other hospital-based physicians.* The DHSS has the authority to regulate the distribution of hospital-based physicians through its approval of all new positions in this area. How does this process operate? Actually, when one studies the distributive-policy-formation machinery of the NHS, it becomes evident that from 1946 to 1970 there was no planning machinery at all. In the candid words of Dr Elizabeth Shore — the head of manpower planning of the DHSS — until 1970, the allocation of human and financial resources was largely based on inertia and the question of who, from the various regions, had more muscle. 'The distribution of doctors by HMC', Shore wrote, 'is most inexact, additions to staffing hitherto being granted largely on the *basis of who shouts loudest*' (my italics).[48] Hooray for candour! The analysis of the distribution of resources by regions made by Noyce, Snaith and Trickey,[49] showing higher expenditure in those regions with a higher proportion of residents from the upper socio-economic groupings in the population, concretely showed just who had the loudest and clearest voice when it came to influencing distributive policy. An analysis of revenues (running costs) received by the ex-RHBs of England and Wales from the central department (DHSS) each year from 1948 to 1970, showed that the allocation per RHB had an inexact relationship to the population served.[50]

How did the pressure (or degree of 'shouting') on distributive policy take place? Through mechanisms built into the structure itself. Indeed, each RHB (and HMC) was allocated a budget, within which it had to operate.[51] And it was up to each HMC, first, and to the RHB afterwards, to make the request for human resources and funds. And, 'the DHSS *normally* agrees to consultant requests within certain numerical limits, but the choice of specialty really originates from the HMC and the RHB. We [the DHSS] don't seek therefore to decide arbitrarily what balance there should be between specialties as this would involve central direction with any mistakes on a national basis having widespread repercussions. We [the DHSS] work on an 'on-demand' basis therefore, within the funds available'.[52,53]

Thus, the allocative planning function took place centrally, but, at least until recently, without any planning or normative criteria, and rather on a 'demand' basis, in which political pressure and muscle directed at the central body by the local pressure groups determined the allocation of resources. Consequently, the regions with the greatest preponderance of classes 1 and 2, and with higher percentages of teaching hospital-based consultants, also were the ones to receive higher proportions of human and financial resources.

In conclusion, the existence of a central system of funding and allocation of resources, as is found in the present NHS, does have an effect on controlling the overall level of health expenditure. But within that overall expenditure, the pattern of distribution of services is the result of a politically-determined 'market' situation in which the amount of political currency allocated for medical resources has depended on the situation of groups and classes within the overall class relations of Britain. It was in 1970 that, for the first time, some measure of need was established, for the purpose of developing a revenue formula which would bear some relationship to the population actually served.[54] This intent of changing the functioning of the central planning machinery away from a pattern of primarily responding to the demands of pressure groups was in reaction to the perceived need for overall economic and social planning discussed in Part II, and was further strengthened by demands for corporate planning in the health sector after the reorganization of the NHS in 1974, as also discussed earlier. That centralization of planning and of the allocation of resources has been further consolidated since 1976 as a consequence of the Great Second Depression of the British economy, which I will discuss later.

2. *General practitioners.* The allocation of general practitioners is controlled by the Medical Practices Committee, created under the Act of 1946. The Medical Practices Committee classifies practice

areas broadly, according to the average size of the list of patients in the area, although other factors are also taken into account. Details of the present classifications, including the list sizes on which they are based, are as follows:[55] (a) *'Designated' areas* (over 2,500 patients per doctor), where special allowances are made to encourage doctors to set up or continue in general practice; (b) *'Open' areas* (2,100 to 2,500 patients), in which admission to the medical list is usually automatic upon submission of a complete application; however, no special allowance is payable; (c) *'Intermediate' areas* (1,800 to 2,100 patients), where admission to the medical list cannot be taken for granted. The Committee considers applications individually and may refuse them if the number of GPs in that area is felt to be already adequate; (d) *'Restricted' areas* (under 1,800 patients), from which all applications are normally refused. This does not stop someone from setting up practice privately, although with a free NHS, private practice is limited, except (to an extent) in the more affluent centres such as London. In 1976, out of a total of 1,469 practice areas, 230 were designated, 362 open, 356 intermediate and 520 were restricted.

3. *Public health physicians.* This group used to be controlled by local authorities. Now renamed, after 1974, community physicians, they are controlled centrally by the DHSS.

Productive intervention policies. Productive intervention policies are those state policies whereby the state directly participates in the production of resources, e.g., medical education in most Western capitalist countries, production of drugs in nationalized drug industries, management of public hospitals, medical research, etc. In all of these activities, the state produces the resources. Before analysing these activities, let me clarify a number of points that have an important bearing on the presentation of these productive activities.

1. The distinction between allocative and productive policies is not always a clear-cut one, and health policies frequently include elements of both.

2. Most allocative functions are administered by the state apparatus, mainly the civil service or the administrative branch of the executive, while productive functions usually take place outside the administrative bodies of the state apparatus. For example, in the production of medical knowledge — research and teaching — the allocative functions are carried out by an administrative branch of

> the state apparatus, while their actual production is carried out by medical schools and research institutions that, although public institutions for the most part, are not directly run by the branch of the state apparatus in charge of the allocative function, nor by any other branch, for that matter.

With this introduction, let us now analyse who decides on the number of human health resources as well as their type, i.e., composition. Before discussing who controls this production, however, let us briefly describe the production process itself. In Great Britain, primary, secondary and higher university education basically come under the jurisdiction of the Department of Education and Science (DES), whose revised budget for 1974-75 amounted to £4,067,000,000, compared with £3,267,000,000 for the DHSS. Reflecting the overwhelming power of the academic community, however, the DES budget is not given directly to the universities but to the University Grants Committee (UGC), 'which acts as an independent buffer between a government department and the universities, so as to avoid central government direction of higher education'.[56] Thus, the UGC acts independently of the DES and certainly of the DHSS, with no government direction as to which disciplines or specialties are to be given priority at any one time.[57]

It is worth stressing that the production of physicians is nationally controlled by the medical schools, with the central government having no real input into the overall number or type of physicians produced. The central government does have, however, some input — in the control of the number (but not type) and distribution of residencies — through the allocative function described earlier. The groups and agencies responsible for the planning and regulation of postgraduate medical education are detailed in Figure 8.1. Indeed, although the DHSS does not control the production of undergraduates, it does, however, have the machinery and leverage to control the nature, type and location (N, T and L) of the postgraduate training posts. One could postulate that the more favourable distribution of hospital physicians than of ambulatory care physicians (general practitioners) in England and Wales is due to the central government control over the former but not over the latter. The distribution of the general practitioners is controlled by the Medical Practices Committee, a subcommittee of the Executive Committee on General Practice that contracts with the DHSS for general practice services.

FIGURE 8.1 *Groups and Agencies Responsible for the Planning and Regulation of Postgraduate Medical Education in England and Wales*

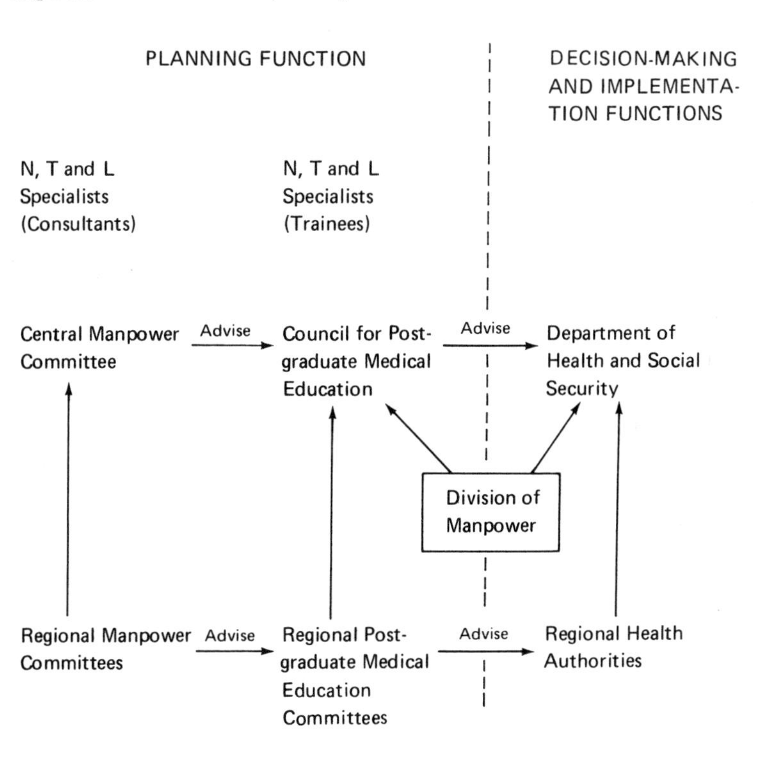

Production of resources: types. Control of the composition of human health resources is in the hands of the medical profession, and particularly of its academic medicine branch. The primary body responsible for stimulating the number and type of physicians is the Council for Postgraduate Medical Education (CPGME), drawing its staff from the manpower division of DHSS, which is autonomous and the primary co-ordinating body for postgraduate medical education in England and Wales. The Council consists of thirty members who represent the Royal Colleges and specialists' associations, teaching staff from undergraduate schools and postgraduate education, as well as DHSS. The Council estimates the overall numbers of existing and required training posts, based on

1. estimates as to the required number of specialists (consultants), prepared by the Central Manpower Committee — another autonomous body, which is in charge of advising the DHSS on numbers and types of medical specialists.
2. estimates as to the number of training jobs available and required, provided by the Regional Postgraduate Medical Education Committees (RPGMECs), the regional equivalents of the Council, which have similar composition at the local level. These committees also advise the Regional Health Authorities (RHAs), the regional branches of the DHSS, in matters pertaining to postgraduate medical education.

The Council (CPGME) and the committees (RPGMECs) provide *advice* to DHSS and its regional bodies, the RHAs. DHSS and the RHAs have the final voice since they must approve all posts, both at the specialist (consultant) and at the training (registrar and below) levels. The Secretary, the top authority of DHSS (and a member of the Cabinet), relies very heavily, however, on the advice of the Council.

The Secretary of DHSS, the manpower division of DHSS, and the RHAs implement the decisions through their responsibilities for approving and funding all training posts. This gives them the leverage to define the distribution of trainees. It seems, however, that DHSS has not used this leverage to redistribute resources and minimize the still very dramatic differences among regions in the U.K. referred to earlier. Only recently, because of the great concern over the maldistribution among specialties, have these bodies started to open trainee positions in those specialties in which they feel there is a great need (e.g., geriatrics), and to slow down and even freeze the opening of others (e.g., neurosurgery).

The reluctance of the DHSS to use the leverage it has to improve the regional distribution of training and specialist posts in the NHS has come about because of the great power of the academic medical establishment, which controls not only the Council but also the Central Manpower Committee. In fact, much has been written, both in the press and in the academic world in the U.K., about the 'medical establishment', which, in Britain, means a very small number of leading medical academicians in the London medical schools who control most of the central committees referred to above. But that control is part of the broader pattern of professional and class control described and detailed earlier in this volume. Regarding the former, let me add a final quotation:

> To think of the medical and health professions as pressure groups working from outside the system is to miss much of the point. The relationship between the central bureaucracy and the health profession is symbiotic. . . . Thus, in the context of the NHS it would probably be fairer to talk about the professionalization of the bureaucracy than the bureaucratization of the medical service.[58]

But this perceptive observer also misses an important point, which is that the symbiosis he refers to is based on the commonality of class origins and class positions of those in both the central bureaucracy and the health profession. And it is that commonality which determines the appropriate scenario for understanding the observed pattern of professional control. As I have shown in the course of this volume, the latter is determined by the former, and not vice versa. This reality does not imply, however, that the top echelons of the civil services and the 'cream' of the medical establishment have uniform interests at all times. Differences may indeed exist. Top civil servants are also subjected to pressure from other power blocs within the capitalist class, and this pressure may conflict with the interests of the medical élite. However, such conflict takes place in the context of an established set of class relations that determines the realm of the possible within the capitalist system. And it is highly unlikely that the nature, composition and distribution of resources in medicine will change at the present historical stage of British capitalism. Such a change will require profound changes in the pattern of class relations in today's Britain.

Notes

1 See, for example, Willcocks, *op. cit.*; and Eckstein, *op. cit.*

2 V. Navarro, 'The Political Economy of Medical Care', *International Journal of Health Services*, 5(1) (1975), pp. 65-94.

3 For a further explanation of the rationality of capitalism, see M. Godelier, *Rationality and Irrationality in Economics*, New York, Monthly Review Press (1973).

4 For an expanded critique of power élite theories, see N. Poulantzas, 'The Problems of the Capitalist State', *New Left Review*, 58 (November - December 1969). Also, 'Economic Elites and Dominant Class', in Miliband, *The State in Capitalist Society, op. cit.*, p. 23.

5 To understand the nature of the state in Western societies, three excellent volumes are: Miliband, *The State in Capitalist Society, op. cit.*: N. Poulantzas, *Political Power and Social Classes*, London, New Left Books (1973); and N. Poulantzas, *Classes in Contemporary Capitalism*, London, New Left Books (1975).

6 Allow me to clarify here that I am aware, of course, of the prevalent belief that as a result of the dramatic expansion of the public sector since World War II (assumedly because of the Keynesian revolution), Western economies, including the British economy, are no longer capitalist but mixed economies. Empirical information shows, however, that in none of our supposedly mixed economies, including the British one, does the state own more than just a subsidiary and complementary part of the means of production.

7 C. Offe, 'The Theory of the Capitalist State and the Problem of Policy Formation', in L. Lindberg, *et al.* (eds.), *Stress and Contradiction in Modern Capitalism*, Lexington, Mass., Lexington Books (1975), p. 126.

8 H. Sigerist, *Landmarks in the History of Hygiene*, London, Oxford University Press (1956).

9 H. Laski, *The State in Theory and Practice*, London, Allen and Unwin (1934), p. 143.

10 Offe, *op. cit.*, p. 127.

11 Navarro, 'Social Class, Political Power and the State and their Implications in Medicine', *op. cit.*

12 Offe, *op. cit.*, p. 126.

13 Gough, *op. cit.*

14 Miliband, *The State in Capitalist Society, op. cit.*

15 T. Lupton and S. Wilson, 'The Social Background and Connections of Top Decision Makers', *The Manchester School*, 27(1) (1959).

16 W.L. Guttsman, *The British Political Elite*, London, MacGibbon and Kee (1963).

17 G.K. Fry, *Statesmen in Disguise*, London, Macmillan (1969).

18 A. Roth, 'The Business Background of MPs', in Urry and Wakeford, *op. cit.*, pp. 131-135.

19 Including chairmen, directors and executives of large business enterprises.

20 Quoted in H. Glennerster and R. Pryke, 'The Contribution of the Public Schools and Oxbridge: 1, Born to Rule, In Urry and Wakeford, *op. cit..*, p. 219.

21 S. Watson, *Oxford Magazine*, (December 1960). Here the public school is a private, fee-paying school, the grammar school is a free, state institution.

22 The function is what determines the class position. See 'Social Classes and their Extended Reproduction', in Poulantzas, *Classes in Contemporary Capitalism, op. cit.*, pp. 13-35.

23 E. Mandel, *Late Capitalism*, London, New Left Books (1975), p. 492.

24 This debate is reproduced in R. Blackburn (ed.), *Ideology in Social Science*, New York, Fontana (1972), pp. 239-262.

25 The number of workers' sons and daughters among the top Swedish politico-bureaucratic echelons was less than 9% in 1961. G. Therborn, 'Power in the Kingdom of Sweden', *International Socialist Journal*, 2 (1965), p. 490.

26 Mandel, *op. cit.*, p. 494.

27 Stanworth and Giddens (eds.), *Elites and Power in British Society*, London, Cambridge University Press (1977).

28 Department of Health and Social Security, *National Health Service Reorganization, op. cit.*

29 For an expansion of the political consequence of economic concentration, see Gough, *op. cit.*

30 V. I. Lenin, *The State and Revolution*, New York, International Publishers (1932).

31 Trilateral Commission, *Governability of Democracies. Report of the Trilateral Task Force*, New York (1975). For an excellent critique of this report, see A. Wolfe, 'Capitalism Shows its Face', *Nation*, 221 (1975), p. 557.

32 A. Wolfe, 'New Directions in Marxist Theory', *Politics and Society*, 4(2) (1974), p. 149.

33 I. Crewe, B. Särlvik and J. Alt, 'Partisan Dealignment in Britain. 1964-1974', *British Journal of Political Science*, 7 (1977), p. 129.

34 T. Forrester, *The Labour Party and the Working Class*, London, Heinemann (1976).

35 In this text, I am using a modified version of Offe's categories. For a presentation of Offe's theories of state intervention, see C. Offe, 'Political Authority and Class Structures — An Analysis of State Capitalist Societies', *International Journal of Sociology*, 2(1) (1972), pp. 73-108. Also, C. Offe, 'The Abolition of Market Control and the Problem of Legitimacy', *Kapitalistate*, 1 (1973), p. 109; and C. Offe and V. Ronge, 'Theses on the Theory of the State', *New German Critique*, 6 (1975), p. 137. For a critique of Offe's work, see S. S. Biermann, V. Christiansen, and K. Dohse, 'Class Domination and the Political System: A Critical Interpretation of Recent Contributions by Claus Offe', *Kapitalistate*, 2 (1973), p. 60; and G.E. Rusconi, 'Marxism in West Germany', and W. Müller and C. Neusüss, 'The Illusion of State Socialism' — both in *Telos*, 25 (1975).

36 For a further expansion of these categories, see Part III in V. Navarro, *Medicine Under Capitalism*, New York, Neale Watson Academic Publications, Inc. (1976).

37 For Lenin's strategy in health services, see 'Leninism and Medicine', in V. Navarro, *Social Security and Medicine in the USSR: A Marxist Critique, op. cit.*

38 For an excellent analysis of the professional dominance in the NHS, see Robson, 'The NHS Company Inc.? The Social Consequence of the Professional Dominance in the National Health Service', *op. cit.*, p. 413. Also, Draper and Smart, *op. cit.*, p. 453.

39 D. Coates, *The Labour Party and the Struggle for Socialism, op. cit.*, p. 48.

40 Special Task Force to the Secretary of Health, Education, and Welfare, *Work in America*, Cambridge, Mass., M.I.T. Press (1973), pp. 77-79.

41 H. Braverman, *op. cit.*

42 Draper and Smart, *op. cit.*

43 Tudor Hart, 'Industry and the Health Service', *op. cit.*, p. 611.

44 Offe, 'The Theory of the Capitalist State and the Problem of Policy Formation', in Lindberg, *et al.* (eds.), *op. cit.*, p. 128.

45 *Ibid.*

46 *Ibid.*

47 The best and most detailed study of the nature of the state and the distribution of power is Miliband, *The State in Capitalist Society, op. cit.*

48 Dr E. Shore, Written communication to the author (1975).

49 J. Noyce, A. H. Snaith, and A. J. Trickey, 'Regional Variations in the Allocation of Financial Resources to the Community Health Services', *The Lancet*, i(7857)(1974), pp. 554-557.

50 Department of Health and Social Security, *Health and Personal Social Services Statistics for England, 1973*, London, Her Majesty's Stationery Office (1973), p. 13.

51 A similar procedure is in effect today with the RHA and AHA, which have been substituted for the RHB and HMC.

52 Shore, *loc. cit.*

53 It is worth clarifying that the DHSS has the power to approve or veto any new position in the hospital sector.

54 Shore, *loc. cit.*

55 *Ibid.*

56 *Ibid.* The UGC is allocated its budgets by the DES in the form of a five-year or quinquennial allocation which provides continuity of planning and also protects universities from the ebbs and flows of government monetary policy.

57 *Ibid.*

58 R. Klein, 'The Political Economy of National Health', *The Public Interest*, 26 (1972), pp. 112-125.

EPILOGUE

The Crisis of British Capitalism in the 1970's and its Implications in Policy Formation in the Health Sector

According to the majority of our media, the Western system of power is in crisis, and within that system, Great Britain is considered to be one of the weakest points. A change of mood in Great Britain has indeed occurred. It was during the post-war boom that most social analysts, with notable exceptions, kept reassuring the British public that class struggles and crises were things of the past, that a new society was appearing in which prosperity and expansion were assured. It was the period of the affluent society, the period of myths, equally experienced on both sides of the Atlantic. And social scientists occupied themselves by covering the so-called leisure problem. Then, in the mid-60's, the shaky basis for that affluence started to crack. The crisis of the British economy — part and parcel of the crisis of the Western capitalist economy — started hitting the front pages of the press, and later, to some degree, started to unsettle the serene ivy walls of Academia. Quick solutions were proposed and in an atmosphere of increased concern, reforms were formulated, all of them aimed at reducing waste in the public sector and making sense out of what was defined, with an earthy touch by an editorial in the *Times*, as 'our present mess'. But those measures, including the 1974 National Health Service reform, proved to be quite insufficient. The cause of the crisis was more profound than initially envisioned by the established centres of power. And new calls for cuts in social expenditure and centralization in the management of the public sector have become the official hallmarks of governmental policy formation. Why those calls? Let us, once again, analyse the nature of the crisis of British capitalism, and within it, the nature of the persistent crisis of the NHS.

The Current Crisis of British Capitalism

What do we mean by crisis? Since 1945, an objective of most Western governments has been to set themselves four basic economic objectives: full employment, economic growth, a balance or surplus in foreign-trade payments, and price stability. It has been common to fail to achieve one out of the four in any given year. But fail in all of them, and we can certainly define the outcome as economic crisis, one that determines a political and ideological crisis as well. Britain is in this situation. Its unemployment is the highest since the Great Depression; its growth has been the slowest among her competitive industrial rivals. The balance of payments had an 'astronomical' deficit of £3828 million in 1974, the highest — tied with Italy — among her industrial competitors; and last but certainly not least, inflation reached 27% in 1975, a record among industrialized capitalist economies.[1] And the Stock Exchange has collapsed. The falls in the principal stock exchanges in 1973 and 1974 were the greatest ever, even greater than the famous Wall Street crash of 1929-1932. The image of the affluent society has indeed been tarnished very rapidly. And questions on the nature of the economic and political system have appeared with nagging consistency, too consistently to guarantee the former comfort of the British establishment. As one of its representatives indicated, 'Something immediately has to be done . . . [including] to call on the armed forces either to provide essential services to the public in areas where these had broken down through economic paralysis or industrial action, or to protect the community from the more violent consequences of a state of hyperinflation — food riots, looting, major demonstrations'.[2]

Why those crises? The most prevalent explanation is that the expansion of the state and its public expenditures has created a shortage of productive capital, i.e., capital that can be used to invest and produce profit. Both through taxes and through public expenditures, the state is assumed to have drained much needed capital. And two items are shown to strengthen that argument: one is the impressive growth of public expenditures in the United Kingdom as a proportion of GNP, from 13% before 1914 to 50% in 1974; and the other is that taxation as a percentage of GNP has risen from 23.2% in 1936 to 48% in 1970.[3] This assumed shift of capital from private to public sectors was supposed to create a shortage of investment capital and a slowing of growth in the private sector, which, in turn, is held to be responsible for the crisis of profitability — the apparent main problem of British capitalism.

This explanation, however, avoids the question raised in this volume of why those public expenditures grew. Indeed, to see that growth without analysing the causes of that growth is to fetishize the state, i.e., to see the state as an independent apparatus that has dynamics of its own. But, as indicated in previous sections, the state is part and parcel of the conflict between Capital and Labour. It mediates that conflict under the hegemony of the former over the latter. In that respect, this growth of the state has to be seen, as indicated before, as a result of the social demands of Labour and needs of Capital. These are the forces that shape the nature of state response, under the hegemony of Capital. And that hegemony appears quite clearly in the present response of the state apparatus to the present crisis of British capitalism, a response that is characterized by:

1. *Aid to private Capital*, with the provision of £180 million in state financing for restructuring industries and stimulating investment. It is worth stressing that, as Fine and Harris have clearly shown, this assistance has been aimed not only at bailing out companies in difficulty, or at feather-bedding employment, but primarily at rationalizing private industry and stimulating investment.[4] That assistance has taken place not only through direct aid, but also, and equally important, by investment incentives, reducing company taxes and, in general, other fiscal policies intended to stimulate the declining rates of profit. That aid, of course, was a consequence of the belief by Conservative and Labour Governments alike that the primordial task of government is to assure the health of the private economy.

2. *Restructuring of the already nationalized industries*, with the proposal of dramatic cuts in employment. The proposal put forward by the Labour Government for the British Steel Corporation, the Central Electricity Generating Board, the British Railways Board, among others, was incumbent upon heavy cuts in employment. It has been the resistance from some segments of the working class that has, on some occasions, as with the Steel Corporation, slowed down or even discontinued those plans.

3. *Cuts in public expenditure*, which have taken place in many different instances, the most prevalent of which was the proposed cut in the

rate of growth of public expenditures from 6% (from 1972 to 1975) to no more than 2¾% for the four years beginning April, 1975.[5] It is worth noting that in this and subsequent proposals put forward by the Labour Government, the cuts have not been uniform across the board. Rather, they have been specifically directed at education, health and housing. But in other areas those cuts have been less extensive and even, in some other areas, like assistance to private industry ('expenditures in trade and industry'), there has been a substantial increase in their proposed rate of growth. Also, by projecting that

TABLE E.1 *The 'Cuts' in Social Expenditure: Percent Change over a Two-year Period at 1976 Prices Excluding the Relative Price Effect*

	Financial Years		
	1971–73	*1973–75*	*1975–77 (projected)*
Personal social services	+32	+17	−11
Health services	+ 9	+ 4	+ 2
Education	+12	+ 3	− 2
Social security	+ 5	+16	+ 8
Housing	+36	+24	− 7
TOTAL SOCIAL SERVICES	+12	+11	+ 1
TOTAL (including food subsidies)	+12	+14	− 1
TOTAL PUBLIC EXPENDITURE(1)	+ 8	+10	− 1
CURRENT v. CAPITAL:			
Current: – personal social services	+28	+25	+ 6
– health	+ 8	+ 7	+ 5
– education	+12	+ 9	+ 1
TOTAL CURRENT (including all other items)	+ 6	+ 8	+ 1
Capital: – personal social services	+59	−25	−54
– health	+17	−15	−28
– education	+10	−28	−36
TOTAL CAPITAL (including all other items)	+10	− 3	−22
CENTRAL v. LOCAL:			
TOTAL central government	+ 4	+13	− 3
TOTAL local government	+15	+ 8	− 9

(1) Including investment grants and debt interest (new basis)
Source: Cmnd. 6721, *The Government's Expenditure Plans*, 2 vols.

the rate of unemployment is going to remain very high, at least until the 1980's, it is expected that the expenditure on unemployment and social security will substantially increase.[6]

This pattern of expenditures appears also in the analysis of capital expenditures. In making the proposed cuts, there was exemption for 'capital expenditures in the nationalized industries ... We also exempted cuts in capital expenditures for support to industry generally. We look at it in that way, and the type of capital expenditure that we are not going ahead with would be on hospitals, school improvements, and those sorts of things'.[7]

In summary, the state response, led by a Labour Government, to the crisis of capitalism has included a most dramatic cut of public expenditures aimed at reducing the proportion of GNP accounted for by public expenditures, with the most heavy cut in the 'welfare state' services, and a shift of part of the capital saved in this way to the private sector, with an increase in public expenditures intended for assisting that sector. Table E.1. summarizes the nature of the cuts in social expenditures. The cuts are both in operating and capital expenditures, and are more substantial in the latter than in the former.

4. *To reduce wages*, by creating unemployment and by establishing an incomes policy, via the 'social contract'. Indeed, it is the policy of both Conservative and Labour Governments to reduce not only the size of the social but also money wages, via an incomes policy that includes primarily a control on the price of labour. Those policies have been particularly successful since 1974, with an actual decline of consumer power of the British working class, and the real take-home pay of workers declining quite substantially over the last two years.[8]

In summary, the capitalist character of the state appears quite clearly in this moment of crisis. The capitalist character of the state appears when its primary aim is the survival and strengthening of the capitalist economy, upon whose health everything else is supposed to depend. Let's see now how that state response has taken place within the NHS.

The Fiscal Crisis of the State and its Implications in the NHS

The expansion of state intervention and state expenditure has required the raising of revenues that are forever insufficient to pay for them. Thus, the continuous fiscal crisis of the state is particularly accentuated in the present conjuncture of crisis of British capitalism. In the previous section, we have discussed the fact that the type of response by the state to this crisis can be summarized as (a) the cutting of social wages, (b) an increasing demand for planning the economy, which requires further centralization in its management, and (c) a growing demand for the rationalization of the system, with more calls for greater productivity and efficiency. As indicated before, the 1974 reorganization of the NHS was the response in the early 1970's to the crisis of British capitalism. But that response proved to be clearly inadequate. Other policies, more stringent ones, were required to put the house of medicine in order. Those policies were:

1. *Cutting the rate of growth of the NHS*, both in operative and capital expenditures, with heavier cuts in the latter than in the former. Table E.1 shows that the most dramatic cuts have been in capital expenditures. Those cuts have affected all sectors of the NHS, including the Health Centres building programmes, whose expenditures are proposed to be reduced from £23 million in 1975-1976 to £17 million in 1979-1980.[9] In toto, the NHS expenditures are supposed to rise 1.8% per year, which is the lowest rate of growth since 1948, when it was established. As indicated in the DHSS document, *Priorities for Health and Personal Social Services*, these cuts are due to the need for reducing public expenditures in order to help the ailing (private) economy.[10]

2. *Changing the order of priorities within the NHS*, with a shift in the pattern of expenditures from costly hospital-based services to less costly community health services. It was proposed, for example, to reduce the rate of growth for acute and general hospital services to 1.2% per year and actually to reduce the expenditure in maternity services by 2% per year, while projecting a further expansion of expenditures to community health services, and most especially for the care of the elderly, mentally and physically retarded and for preventive services. The rationale for the expansion for those last types of service includes as a primary concern cost saving, as indicated in the document, *Prevention and Health: Everybody's Business*, which states that, 'Prevention and health education are particularly important when resources are tightly limited as they can often lead to savings in resources in other areas . . .'.[11]

Thus, emphasis is placed not only on reducing overall expenditures of the NHS but also on establishing a new pattern of expenditures which shifts away from the costly hospital-based care to the development of alternative strategies of health services that, besides being more responsive to the community needs and to the needs of special constituencies such as the elderly and the handicapped, will also be, in the long run, cheaper. It is important to stress, however, that, while the DHSS has control over the hospital sector, it has no control over the expenditures of the local authorities, whose social departments are the ones primarily responsible for the care of the elderly and handicapped. It is because of this situation that, while a slower rate of growth in the hospital sector is likely to occur, the expansion in the care expenditures for those segments of the population in need, like the elderly and handicapped, is questionable. Indeed, the only direct control that the central government has over local authority services is to sanction the borrowing of capital expenditures. Otherwise, the DHSS is unable to directly influence the way in which local authorities arrange their contribution to caring services. A survey of the social services department carried out by the British Association of Social Workers showed that, in their 1976-1977 budgets, many local authorities were cutting back on *exactly those services that had been given high priority by the DHSS Consultative document.* It was estimated that services for the elderly, mentally handicapped and mentally ill were cut by £5 million nationally.[12] Seeing the state intervention *in toto*, then, the state response has been to reduce not only hospital services but also the alternative types of care that could have proven to be less expensive.

3. *An increased centralization and strengthening of the planning apparatus of the NHS*, with the development of strategies and methodologies to correct the regional imbalances in the NHS resources.[13] The year 1976 marked the formal introduction of the new NHS planning system. Established two years after the reorganization of 1974, this system was perceived as necessary for further centralization of the allocation of resources.[14] Side by side with the establishment of this system, there was a development of criteria for the allocation of resources, criteria established with a heavy input from academic medicine,[15] which determined a set of social class and professional biases in the criteria. For example, one influential idea in setting up those criteria was the prevalent belief

held by many in academe that inequalities of consumption among different social classes had been corrected by the welfare state measures and, instead, 'new' inequities still persisted that merited attention, such as inequities of consumption among regions, among age groups and among types of care. Reflecting those beliefs, the formula used to establish the criteria for allocating resources included weighting factors for regional and age differentials of consumption and for overall mortality (as proxy of need, expressing also the biases of epidemiologists), but did not include a weighting factor for social class. As Lee indicates, this formula shows more concern about geographical than social class differences in accessibility of resources.[16] Class and professional biases do indeed appear in the establishment of that planning system and its allocative criteria.

4. *Exploring the possibility of expanding the charges paid by the public for individual treatment*, in order to, as Crossman used to say, 'look for alternative sources of revenues less dependent on the chancellor's whims'.[17] It is worth mentioning in this regard that the increase of those charges has also been justified by Conservative and Labour politicians as a way of making the populace more aware of the value of care. None other than the then Secretary of the DHSS, Sir Keith Joseph, indicated that 'increased dental charges . . . would give a financial incentive to patients to look after their teeth . . . They would therefore have a beneficial effect on dental health'.[18] As Tudor Hart has noticed, that rationale could very well lead to governments raising the tax on coffins to reduce mortality.[19]

5. *Emphasizing the individual's responsibility for care*, with a focus on public and private pronouncements which would declare that the most important improvement in the health of the individual is likely to appear from changes in individual behaviour. As indicated in the *Priorities* document:

> The primary responsibility for his own health falls on the individual. The role of the health profession and of government is limited to ensuring that the public have access to such knowledge as is available about the importance of personal habit on health and at the very least no obstacles are placed in the way of those who decide to act on that knowledge.[20]

Needless to say, this emphasis on individual as different from collective responsibility has an ideological function. It legitimizes the absence of public response to individual needs. In the words of one of its popularizers in the U.S., ex-President Nixon, 'Do not ask what government can do for you, ask what you can do for yourself'. The individual is held to be primarily responsible for his or her health, wealth and future.

Final Remarks

As I have indicated in this volume, if we are to understand past and present policy formation in the British health sector, or any other sector for that matter, we have to understand, first, the distribution of power in Great Britain and, second, the nature, role and instrumentality of the state. This understanding leads us to realize (a) that social class is a necessary category in comprehending the distribution of power in Great Britain, and (b) that class struggle is a most relevant paradigm for understanding the nature of Great Britain and its health sector, thus confirming the veracity of Marx and Engels' dictum that class struggle is the main motor of history and, as I have shown in this volume, of health and social legislation as well. That class struggle in Britain has been a long and heart-breaking one, doubly painful because the militancy of the working class has constantly been diluted and de-emphasized by the timid leadership of the Labour Party. A gap has continuously existed between the demands of the working class, frequently presented in Labour Movement declarations, and the policies generated by successive Labour Governments. As Townsend recently indicated, Labour Governments 'tend to compromise too readily with entrenched interests, avoiding the need to confront racial and social prejudice with moral authority, failing to introduce institutional change . . .'[21] It would be an error, however, to think such behaviour of Labour Governments is a result of the moral cowardice, weakness or turpitude of their leaders. Rather, that behaviour is the result of the Labour leaders' commitment to capitalism, a commitment documented in this volume. Consequently, the changes which have taken place under Labour Governments *have not represented an alternative but an adaptation to capitalism.* As Miliband eloquently stated:

> To assume personalities are the problem would be to engage in a crude and sentimental demonology, which conceals the real issue. The trouble does not lie in the wishes and intentions of powerholders, but in the fact that the reformers, with or without inverted commas, are the prisoners, and usually the willing prisoners, of an economic and social framework which necessarily turns their reforming proclamations, however sincerely meant, into verbiage.[22]

I have tried to show in this volume that the Labour Governments' policies have not been aimed at transforming or transcending Great Britain's economic and social framework. For example, we have seen how health and social policies were implemented on the condition that they would not hurt or damage the state of the economy, on whose health everything and everyone assumedly depends. The survival and strengthening of capitalism were and are the first and foremost goals of Labour Governments. As one of Labour's Prime Ministers, James Callaghan, once said, 'A Labour Government must not rush its fences ... Its first job must be to restore the economy. Then, we can start paying ourselves a dividend'.[23] Also, because of that commitment to save the (capitalist) economy, we have seen that all health and social policies, from the creation of the NHS in 1948 to its reform in 1974, took place within the pattern of power determined by class relations in Great Britain.

Yet because of the actual and potential militancy of the working class, far readier for changes than the leadership of the Labour Party, that leadership had to legitimize itself by calls — particularly at election time — for socialism and the creation of a classless society. As Saville indicated:

> How it comes about that those who win elections with socialist phrases on their lips — and most are not conscious hypocrites — and then proceed to administer a capitalist society, which they have previously denounced in an as efficient way as possible, is one of the central ironies of modern British history.[24]

To summarize, the aim of the Labour Party is not to achieve a socialist transformation of British society. This position explains why the Labour policies are directed primarily at running the economy (capitalism) better. Socialism, then, is presented as a theory of management rather than a revolutionary praxis. Consequently, the Labour Party has historically de-emphasized all mass mobilization, focusing, instead, on the parliamentarian road as the exclusive road to change, without significantly altering the pattern of class relations in today's Great Britain.

If, however, we are to understand socialism as the 'process towards the self-government of the masses',[25] then the Labour Party is as far away from socialism as the Vatican is from the Sermon on the Mount. The Labour Party's commitment to the survival and strengthening of capitalism, with the set of class relations capitalism determines, makes that profound democratization of British society unattainable, as the health and social policies described in this volume prove. The NHS — a victory for the working class — has not been an instrument for the self-realization of the masses, whereby they are the agents and not the subjects of change within and outside the health sector. For that democratization of the British social, political and economic spheres — the goals and objectives of the labouring classes — to take place, a political commitment to transcend capitalism, the social formation in Great Britain today, is needed, a commitment far more profound and consistent than the Labour Party represents.

On this note, then, I end this volume. Needless to say, the interpretation of British society and its medicine as presented here represents a minority voice in English literature. It is in conflict with most prevalent explanations of the health sector in Great Britain, which are mere apologetic forms for class relations in today's Great Britain. Still, the veracity of this interpretation will be affirmed not by its 'popularity' in the corridors of power or academic life, which will be nil, but, to use a Gramscian expression, on the terrain of praxis and history. Because of this I dedicate this volume to those in Britain who are struggling for that socialist change.

NOTES

1 All these figures are from A. Gamble and P. Walton, *op. cit.*

2 *The Times* (August 16, 1974).

3 Gamble and Walton, *op. cit.*, p. 27.

4 Fine and Harris, *op. cit.*, p. 3.

5 White Paper, *Public Expenditures to 1978-1979*, Command Paper 5879, London, Her Majesty's Stationery Office (1975).

6 Fine and Harris, *op. cit.*, p. 21.

7 Quoted in Fine and Harris, *op. cit.*, from the *Ninth Report of Public Expenditure Committee*, Question 105.

8 Gamble and Walton, *op. cit.*, p. 189.

9 Department of Health and Social Security, *Priorities for Health and Personal Social Services in England*, London, Her Majesty's Stationery Office (1976).

10 *Ibid.*

11 Department of Health and Social Security, *Prevention and Health: Everybody's Business*, London, Her Majesty's Stationery Office (1976).

12 British Association of Social Workers (1975-1976), press release.

13 Department of Health and Social Security, *The First Interim Report of the Resource Allocation Working Party*, London, Her Majesty's Stationery Office (1975).

14 Department of Health and Social Security, *Health Services Management. The NHS Planning System: Planning Activities in 1967-1977*, London, Her Majesty's Stationery Office (1976), p. 30.

15 Resource Allocation Working Party, *Sharing Resources for Health in England*, London, Her Majesty's Stationery Office (1976).

16 K. Lee, 'Public Expenditure, Planning and Local Democracy', in K. Barnard and K. Lee (eds.), *Conflicts in the National Health Service, op. cit.*, p. 223.

17 R.H.S. Crossman, *Paying for Social Services*, London, The Fabian Society (1969).

18 *The Guardian* (February 3, 1971).

19 J. Tudor Hart, *The NHS in England and Wales. A Marxist Perspective* (mimeograph).

20 Department of Health and Social Security, *Priorities for Health and Personal Social Services in England, op. cit.*, pp. 62-63.

21 B. Abel-Smith, P. Townsend, R. Titmuss, and R.H.S. Crossman, *Socialism and Affluence: Four Fabian Essays*, London, The Fabian Society (1967), p. 68.

22 Miliband, *The State in Capitalist Society, op. cit.*

23 '1963 T.U.C. Gathering', *The Guardian*, 4 September 1963.

24 J. Saville, 'Labourism and the Labour Government', *Socialist Register 1967*, London, Merlin Press (1967), p. 53.

25 V.I. Lenin, *Selected Works*, Vol. III, New York, International Publishers (1967).

Bibliography

B. Abel-Smith, *The Hospitals, 1800-1948*, London, Heinemann (1964).

B. Abel-Smith, P. Townsend, R. Titmuss, and R.H.S. Crossman, *Socialism and Affluence: Four Fabian Essays*, London, The Fabian Society (1967).

W. Abendroth, *A Short History of the European Working Class*, New York, Monthly Review Press (1972).

O. Anderson, *Health Care: Can There Be Equity? The United States, Sweden and England*, New York, John Wiley and Sons (1972).

P. Anderson, 'Origins of the Present Crises', *New Left Review*, 23 (1964).

R.P. Arnot, *General Strike, May 1926: Its Origin and History*, New York, Augustus M. Kelley (1967).

C.R. Attlee, *As it Happened*, London, Heinemann (1954).

K. Barnard and K. Lee (eds.), *Conflicts in the National Health Service*, London, Croom Helm (1977).

R. Battistella and T. Chester, 'The 1974 Reorganization of the British National Health Service — Aims and Issues', *New England Journal of Medicine*, 289(12): 610-615 (1973).

R. Battistella and T. Chester, 'Reorganization of the National Health Service: Background and Issues in England's Quest for a Comprehensive-Integrated Planning and Delivery System', *Health and Society*, 51(4): 526-527 (1973).

F. Bealey and H. Pelling, *Labour and Politics, 1900-1906*, London, Macmillan (1958).

J.L. Berlant, *Profession and Monopoly. A Study of Medicine in the United States and Great Britain*, Berkeley, University of California Press (1975).

W. Beveridge, *Report on Social Insurance and Allied Services*, London, His Majesty's Stationery Office (1942).

S.S. Biermann, V. Christiansen, and K. Dohse, 'Class Domination and the Political System: A Critical Interpretation of Recent Contributions by Claus Offe', *Kapitalistate*, 2: 60 (1973).

I. Blair, 'Private Practice. Notes on a Growth Industry', *Medicine in Society*, 1(3): 42 (1974).

R. Blackburn (ed.), *Ideology in Social Science*, New York, Fontana (1972).

N. Bosanquet, 'Inequalities in the Health Service', *New Society*, 17(450): 809-812 (1971).

R.A. Brady, *Crisis in Britain: Plans and Achievements of the Labour Government*, London, Cambridge University Press (1950).

H. Braverman, *Labour and Monopoly Capital*, New York, Monthly Review Press (1974).

British Gazette, May 10, 1926.

British Medical Association, *A General Medical Service for the Nation*, London, BMA (1938).

J. Brotherston, 'Evolution of Medical Practice', in G. McLachlan and T. McKeown (eds.), *Medical History and Medical Care*, Oxford, Oxford University Press (1971).

M. Barrett Brown and K. Coates (eds.), *Trade Union Register, 3*, London, Spokesman Books (1973).

R.G.S. Brown, *The Changing National Health Service*, London, Routledge and Kegan Paul (1973).
D.E. Butler and A. King, *The British General Election of 1964*, London, Macmillan (1965).
D.E. Butler and A. King, *The British General Election of 1966*, London, Macmillan (1966).
D.E. Butler and R. Rose, *The British General Election of 1959*, London, Macmillan (1960).
J. Butler, *Family Doctors and Public Policy*, London, Routledge and Kegan Paul (1973).
J. Cairns, 'The Cancer Problem', *Scientific American*, 233 (1975).
A.M. Carr-Saunders and P.A. Wilson, *The Professions, Part I*, Oxford, Clarendon Press (1933).
A. Cartwright and R. Marshall, 'General Practice in 1963: Its Conditions, Contents and Satisfactions', *Medical Care*, 3(2): 69-87 (1965).
M. Castells, *The Urban Question*, London, Edward Arnold Publishers, Ltd. (1977).
B. Castle, *NHS Revisited*, London, The Fabian Society (Tract No. 440) (1976).
T. Chester, 'Public Money in the Private Sector', *National Westminster Bank Review* (May, 1973).
Child Poverty Action Group, *Poverty and the Labour Government*, London, CPAG (1970).
B. Coates and E. Rawstron, *Regional Variations in Britain*, London, B.T. Batsford (1971).
D. Coates, *The Labour Party and the Struggle for Socialism*, London, Cambridge University Press (1975).
A.L. Cochrane, *Effectiveness and Efficiency: Random Reflections on Health Services*, London, Nuffield Provincial Hospitals Trust (1972).
G.D.H. Cole and R. Postgate, *The British Common People, 1746-1946*, London, Methuen and Company (1961).
M. Cole (ed.), *Beatrice Webb's Diaries, 1924-1932*, London, Longman, Green and Company (1956).
Consultative Council on Medical and Allied Services, *Interim Report on the Future Position of Medical and Allied Services*, London, His Majesty's Stationery Office (1920).
L. Cowen, 'Liberty, Laissez-Faire and Licensure in Nineteenth Century Britain', *Bulletin of the History of Medicine*, 43, (1969).
I. Crewe, B. Särlvik and J. Alt, 'Partisan Dealignment in Britain. 1964-1974', *British Journal of Political Science*, 7: 129 (1977).
W.H. Crook, *The General Strike*, Chapel Hill, University of North Carolina Press (1931).
A. Crosland, *The Future of Socialism*, London, Jonathan Cape, Ltd. (1956).
R.H.S. Crossman, *Paying for Social Services*, London, The Fabian Society (1969).
P. Deane and W. A. Cole, *British Economic Growth, 1688-1959*, London, Cambridge University Press (1967).
Department of Health and Social Security, *Democracy in the National Health Service*, London, Her Majesty's Stationery Office (1974).
Department of Health and Social Security, *The First Interim Report of the Resource Allocation Working Party*, London, Her Majesty's Stationery Office (1975).
Department of Health and Social Security, *Health and Personal Social Services Statistics for England, 1973*, London, Her Majesty's Stationery Office (1973).
Department of Health and Social Security, *Health Services Management. The NHS Planning System: Planning Activities in 1967-1977*, London, Her Majesty's Stationery Office (1976).

Department of Health and Social Security, *National Health Service: The Future Structure of the NHS*, London, Her Majesty's Stationery Office (1970).
Department of Health and Social Security, *National Health Service Reorganization*, London, Her Majesty's Stationery Office (Command Paper 5055) (1972).
Department of Health and Social Security, *National Health Service Reorganization: Consultative Document*, London, Her Majesty's Stationery Office (1971).
Department of Health and Social Security, *National Health Service Twentieth Anniversary Conference Report*, London, Her Majesty's Stationery Office (1968).
Department of Health and Social Security, *Prevention and Health: Everybody's Business*, London, Her Majesty's Stationery Office (1976).
Department of Health and Social Security, *Priorities for Health and Personal Social Services in England*, London, Her Majesty's Stationery Office (1976).
P. Draper and T. Smart, 'Social Science and Health Policy in the United Kingdom: Some Contributions of the Social Sciences to the Bureaucratization of the National Health Service', *International Journal of Health Services*, 4(3): 453-470 (1974).
H. Eckstein, *The English Health Service: Its Origins, Structure and Achievement*, Cambridge, Harvard University Press (1959).
The Economist (November, 1945), (January 15, 1966).
C. Farman, *May 1926. The General Strike*, London, Panther Books (1974).
B. Fine and L. Harris, 'The British Economy: May 1975 — January 1976', *Bulletin of the Conference of Socialist Economists*, V:1 (October, 1976).
P. Florence, *Ownership, Control and Success of Large Companies: An Analysis of English Industrial Structure and Policy, 1936-1951*, London, Sweet and Maxwell (1961).
T. Forrester, *The Labour Party and the Working Class*, London, Heinemann (1976).
G. Forsyth, *Doctors and State Medicine: A Study of the British Health Service*, New York, J.B. Lippincott Company (1966).
G. Forsyth, 'Introduction', in J. Van Langendonck, *Prelude to Harmony on a Community Theme. Health Care Insurance Policies in the Six and Britain*, Oxford, Oxford University Press (1975).
H. Frankel, *Capitalist Society and Modern Sociology*, Surrey, Lawrence and Wishart (1970).
G.K. Fry, *Statesmen in Disguise*, London, Macmillan (1969).
A. Gamble and P. Walton, *Capitalism in Crisis: Inflation and the State*, New York, Macmillan (1976).
V. George and P. Wilding, 'Social Values, Social Class, and Social Policy', *Social and Economic Administration*, 6(3): 236-248 (1972).
B.B. Gilbert, *The Evolution of National Insurance in Great Britain. The Origins of the Welfare State*, London, Michael Joseph (1976).
D.G. Gill, 'The British National Health Service: Professional Determinants of Administrative Structure', *International Journal of Health Services*, 1(4): 342-353 (1971).
A. Glyn and B. Sutcliffe, *British Capitalism, Workers, and the Profit Squeeze*, London, Penguin (1972).
M. Godelier, *Rationality and Irrationality in Economics*, New York, Monthly Review Press (1973).
I. Gough, 'State Expenditure in Advanced Capitalism', *New Left Review*, 92:63 (1975).
P. Gregg, *The Welfare State*, London, George G. Harrap (1967).
H. Grundwald, 'Safety and Health at Work', *Comment*, 2(21) (1973).
W.L. Guttsman, *The British Political Elite*, London, MacGibbon and Kee (1963).
J. Hallan, *CHCs in Action*, London, Nuffield Provincial Hospitals Trust (1976).
E.C. Hammond, 'Epidemiologic Basis for Cancer Prevention', *Cancer*, 33(6) (1974).

J. Tudor Hart, 'Bevan and the Doctors', *The Lancet*, ii(7839): 1196-1197 (1973).
J. Tudor Hart, 'Industry and the Health Service', *The Lancet*, ii(7829):611 (1973).
J. Tudor Hart, 'The Inverse Care Law', *The Lancet*, i(7696): 405-412 (1971).
J. Tudor Hart, 'A New Kind of Doctor', *International Journal of Health Services* (in process).
J. Tudor Hart, *The NHS in England and Wales. A Marxist Perspective* (mimeograph).
J. Tudor Hart, 'Primary Care in the Industrial Areas of Britain', *International Journal of Health Services*, 2(3): 349-366 (1972).
J. Tudor Hart, 'Reform and Reaction in Medical Care', *International Journal of Health Services*, 2(4): 567-574 (1972).
D. Harvey, *Social Justice and the City*, London, Edward Arnold Publishers, Ltd. (1973).
I. Illich, *Medical Nemesis: The Expropriation of Health*, London, Calder and Boyars (1975).
D. Irvine and M. Jefferys, 'BMA Planning Unit Survey of General Practice, 1969', *British Medical Journal* (November 4, 1971).
S. Jonas and D. Banta, 'The 1974 Reorganization of the British National Health Service: An Analysis', *Journal of Community Health*, 1(2): 91-105 (1975).
T.J. Jones, *Lloyd George*, New York, Random House (1951).
L.A. Jordan, 'Theory of Social Class', *Karl Marx, Economy, Class and Social Revolution*, New York, Scribner's and Sons (1971).
P. Kinnersly, *The Hazards of Work*, London, Pluto Press (1973).
R. Klein, 'The Political Economy of National Health', *Public Interest*, 26: 112-125 (1972).
R. Klein and J. Lewis, 'The Politics of Consumer Representatives. A Study of Community Health Councils', London, Centre for Studies in Social Policy (1976).
R. Kohn, 'The Reorganization of the British National Health Service: A Largely Frustrated Case Study', *International Journal of Health Services* (in process).
J. Kuczynski, *A Short History of Labour Conditions Under Industrial Capitalism, Volume I*, London, Frederick Muller, Ltd. (1942).
Labour Party, *Annual Conference Report*, London (1918, 1934, 1945 and 1959).
G. Lampedusa, *The Leopard*, New York, Random House (1960).
H. Laski, *The Crisis and the Constitution*, London, Hogarth Press (1932).
H. Laski, *The State in Theory and Practice*, London, Allen and Unwin (1934).
A. Learmonth, *Health*, London, Open Univeristy Press (1972).
J.A.H. Lee, S.L. Morrison and J.M. Morris, 'Fatality from Three Common Regional Conditions in Teaching and Non-Teaching Hospitals', *The Lancet*, ii:785 (19 October 1957).
J.R. Lee, *Life of Adam Smith*, New York, Augustus M. Kelley (1965).
V.I. Lenin, *The State and Revolution*, Vol. III, New York, International Publishers (1932).
V.I. Lenin, *Selected Works*, Vol. III, New York, International Publishers (1967).
A. Levinson, *The Working Class Majority*, New York, Coward, McCann and Geoghegan, Inc. (1974).
R. Levitt, *The Reorganized National Health Service*, London, Holmes and Meier (1976).
S.S. Lewis, 'Nurses and Trade Unions in Britain', *International Journal of Health Services*, 6(4): 641-649 (1976).
S.M. Lipset, *The First New Nation: The United States in Historical and Comparative Perspective*, New York, Basic Books (1963).
T. Lupton and S. Wilson, 'The Social Background and Connections of Top Decision Makers', *The Manchester School*, 27(1) (1959).

R.W. Lyman, *The First Labour Government, 1924*, London, Chapman and Hall (1953).
E. Mandel, *Late Capitalism*, London, New Left Books (1975).
S.A. Margolies, 'What Do Bosses Do? The Origins and Functions of Hierarchy in Capitalist Production', *The Review of Radical Political Economics*, 6(2): 60-112 (1974).
K. Marx, *Capital*, Vol. III, New York, International Publishers (1965).
K. Marx and F. Engels, *The Communist Manifesto*, New York, International Publishers (1960).
D. McKie, 'Labour and the NHS', *The Lancet*, ii(7833): 841 (1973).
R. Miliband, *Parliamentary Socialism*, London, Merlin Press (1973).
R. Miliband, *The State in Capitalist Society*, London, Weidenfeld and Nicolson (1970).
Ministry of Health, *A National Health Service*, London, His Majesty's Stationery Office (Command Paper 6502) (1944).
Ministry of Health, *National Health Service: The Administrative Structure of the Medical and Related Services in England and Wales*, London, Her Majesty's Stationery Office (1968).
C.L. Mowat, *Britain Between the Wars, 1918-1940*, London, Methuen (1968).
W. Müller and C. Neusüss, 'The Illusion of State Socialism', *Telos*, 25 (1975).
D.S. Murray, *Why a National Health Service? The Part Played by the Socialist Medical Association*. London, Pemberton Books (1971).
T. Nairn, 'The British Political Elite', *New Left Review*, 23 (1964).
T. Nairn, 'The English Working Class', *New Left Review*, 24 (1964).
V. Navarro, *Medicine Under Capitalism*, New York, Neale Watson Academic Publications, Inc. (1976).
V. Navarro, 'The Political Economy of Medical Care', *International Journal of Health Services*, 5(1): 65-94 (1975).
V. Navarro, 'Social Class, Political Power and the State and their Implications in Medicine', *Social Science and Medicine*, 10(9/10) (1976).
V. Navarro, 'Social Policy Issues: An Explanation of the Composition, Nature and Functions of the Present Health Sector of the United States', *Bulletin of the New York Academy of Medicine*, 51(1): 199-234 (1975).
V. Navarro, *Social Security and Medicine in the USSR: A Marxist Critique*, Lexington, Mass., Lexington Books/D.C. Heath (1977).
Needle, 'The Way Forward for Health Workers', 12 (1972).
J. Noyce, A.H. Snaith and A.J. Trickey, 'Regional Variations in the Allocation of Financial Resources to the Community Health Services', *The Lancet*, i(7857): 554-557 (1974).
O.E.C.D., *Expenditure Trends in O.E.C.D. Countries, 1960-1980*, (1972).
C. Offe, 'The Abolition of Market Control and the Problem of Legitimacy', *Kapitalistate*, 1:109 (1973).
C. Offe, 'Political Authority and Class Structures — An Analysis of State Capitalist Societies', *International Journal of Sociology*, 2(1): 73-108 (1972).
C. Offe, 'The Theory of the Capitalist State and the Problem of Policy Formation', in L. Lindberg, *et al.* (eds.) *Stress and Contradiction in Modern Capitalism*, Lexington, Mass., Lexington Books/D.C. Heath (1975).
C. Offe and V. Ronge, 'Theses on the Theory of the State', *New German Critique*, 6:137 (1975).
A. Porritt, *A Review of the Medical Services in Great Britain: Report of a Medical Review Committee Established by the British Medical Association and the Various Consultant Colleges Under the Chairmanship of Sir Arthur Porritt*, London, British Medical Association (1962).

N. Poulantzas, *Classes in Contemporary Capitalism*, London, New Left Books (1975).
N. Poulantzas, 'Marxist Political Theory in Great Britain', *New Left Review*, 43 (1968).
N. Poulantzas, *Political Power and Social Classes*, London, New Left Books (1973).
N. Poulantzas, 'The Problems of the Capitalist State', *New Left Review*, 58 (1969).
Radical Statistics Health Group, *Whose Priorities?*, London (1976).
J.C.W. Reith, *Into the Wind*, London, Hodder and Stoughton (1949).
Resource Allocation Working Party, *Sharing Resources for Health in England*, London, Her Majesty's Stationery Office (1976).
J. Robson, 'History and the Robens Report', *Medicine in Society*, 1(3): 10 (1974).
J. Robson, 'The NHS Company Inc.? The Social Consequence of the Professional Dominance in the National Health Service', *International Journal of Health Services*, 3(3): 413-426 (1973).
Royal College of Surgeons, *Evidence of the Royal College of Surgeons to the Royal Commission on Doctors' and Dentists' Remuneration*, London, Her Majesty's Stationery Office (1958).
Royal Commission on Doctors' and Dentists' Remuneration, *Report to Parliament, February, 1960*, London, Her Majesty's Stationery Office (Command Paper 939) (1960).
Royal Commission on Local Government in England, *Report, Volume 1*, London, Her Majesty's Stationery Office (Command Paper 4040) (1968).
Royal Commission on National Health Insurance, *Report*, London, His Majesty's Stationery Office (Command Paper 2596) (1926).
Royal Commission on the Poor Laws and the Relief of Distress, *Minority Report*, London, His Majesty's Stationery Office (Command Paper 4499) (1909).
G.E. Rusconi, 'Marxism in West Germany', *Telos*, 25 (1975).
J. Saville, 'Labourism and the Labour Government', *The Socialist Register 1967*, London, Merlin Press (1967).
E.W. Saward (ed.), *The Regionalization of Personal Health Services*, London, Prodist (1975).
G.B. Shaw, *The Doctor's Dilemma*, London, Constable (1930).
G.B. Shaw (ed.), *Essays on Fabian Socialism*, London, Constable (1931).
E. Shore, written communication to the author (1975).
H. Sigerist, *Landmarks in the History of Hygiene*, London, Oxford University Press (1956).
H. Sigerist, *Medicine and Health in the Soviet Union*, New York, Citadel Press (1947).
M.A. Simpson, *Medical Education: A Critical Approach*, London, Butterworths (1972).
Special Task Force to the Secretary of Health, Education, and Welfare, *Work in America*, Cambridge, Mass., M.I.T. Press (1973).
M. Stacey (ed.), *The Sociology of the NHS*, Sociological Review Monograph, University of Keele (1976).
Stanworth and Giddens (eds.), *Elites and Power in British Society*, London, Cambridge University Press (1977).
R. Stevens, *Medical Practice in Modern England: The Impact of Specialization and State Medicine*, New Haven, Conn., Yale University Press (1966).
M Stewart, *Unpaid Public Science*, London, Fabian Pamphlet, No. 3 (1964).
M. Susser, 'Ethical Components in the Definition of Health', *International Journal of Health Services*, 4(3): 539-548 (1974).
M. Taylor, 'NHS Reorganization, An Opportunity for Democratic Control?' in M.

Barrett Brown and K. Coates (eds.), *Trade Union Register, 3*, London, Spokesman Books (1973).
M. Terris, 'Crisis and Change in America's Health System', *American Journal of Public Health*, 63(4): 313-318 (1973).
E.P. Thompson, 'The Peculiarities of the English', in R. Miliband and J. Saville (eds.), *The Socialist Register, 1965*, London, Merlin Press (1965).
G. Therborn, 'Power in the Kingdom of Sweden', *International Socialist Journal*, 2 (1965).
R.M. Titmuss, *Birth, Poverty and Wealth*, London, Hamilton Medical Books (1943).
P. Townsend and N. Bosanquet (eds.), *Labour and Inequality*, London, The Fabian Society (1972).
Trades Union Congress General Council, *The Mining Crisis and the National Strike*, London (1927).
Trilateral Commission, *Governability of Democracies. Report of the Trilateral Task Force*, New York (1975).
J. Urry and J. Wakeford (eds.), *Power in Britain: Sociological Readings*, London, Heinemann (1973).
S. Watson, *Oxford Magazine*, London (December, 1960).
D. Wedderburn, 'Facts and Theories of the Welfare State', *The Socialist Register, 1965,* London, Merlin Press (1965).
J. Westergaard and H. Resler, *Class in a Capitalist Society. A Study of Contemporary Britain*, London, Heinemann (1975).
White Paper, *Public Expenditures to 1978-1979*, London, Her Majesty's Stationery Office (Command Paper 5879) (1975).
D. Widgery, 'Unions and Strikes in the National Health Service in the United Kingdom', *International Journal of Health Services*, 6(2): 301-308 (1976).
A.J. Willcocks, *The Creation of the National Health Service: A Study of Pressure Groups and a Major Social Policy Decision*, London, Routledge and Kegan Paul (1973).
H. Wilson, *The House of Commons, Volume 629*, London, Hansard (Fifth Series) (1960).
A. Wolfe, 'Capitalism Shows its Face', *Nation*, 221: 557 (1975).
A. Wolfe, 'New Directions in Marxist Theory', *Politics and Society*, 4(2):149 (1974).

Index